Mbeleck Mandenge

Whither Kamerun

Mbeleck Mandenge

Whither Kamerun

Brutality as a Mode of Governance

Dictus Publishing

Imprint
Any brand names and product names mentioned in this book are subject to trademark, brand or patent protection and are trademarks or registered trademarks of their respective holders. The use of brand names, product names, common names, trade names, product descriptions etc. even without a particular marking in this work is in no way to be construed to mean that such names may be regarded as unrestricted in respect of trademark and brand protection legislation and could thus be used by anyone.

Cover image: www.ingimage.com

Publisher:
Dictus Publishing
is a trademark of
International Book Market Service Ltd., member of OmniScriptum Publishing Group
17 Meldrum Street, Beau Bassin 71504, Mauritius

Printed at: see last page
ISBN: 978-613-7-35002-7

INTRODUCTION

Colonialism is a political doctrine which seeks to justify the exploitation of a territory or state by a foreign state; the sovereignty that the colonising entity exercises on its colony is translated by political domination (an administration and a governor in place), military and economic control to the detriment of the local people. The driving forces of colonialism are various.

In Hobson's (1965) view, colonialism derived from the attempt to find new markets for investments, as the capacity for production expanded beyond what could possibly be sold in the markets. According to him, the majority of the population are only able to afford to buy a relatively small proportion of the goods that can be produced. So, there is a constant striving both for new markets in which to sell and for ways of cheapening production by finding sources of inexpensive raw materials and labour power in other parts of the world. Specific other motives of the colonialists could be summarised as follows:
- The demand for tropical products such as palm oil and cotton as inputs to the manufacture of cheap soap, margarine and textiles
- Strategic territory-grabbing by Europeans powers who were in competition with each other for the resources of these lands
- Space for population surplus of the *métropole*
- Control of commercial routes to ensure their security
- Prevention of the expansion of competing powers

A common view is that Europeans set out to colonise the world as part of a "civilising mission." The big colonial powers like Spain, Portugal, Britain, and France for long, thought of themselves as being of their duty as civilised countries.

The term "neo-colonialism" derives from colonialism. Beginning from the 1960s, it designates various efforts (overt and covert) of a former colonial power to continue to control a people in the domains of economy and politics after having granted them formal independence.

After several years of struggle, Kwame Nkrumah and fellow Ghanaian nationalists could pop champagnes to celebrate their triumph on the 6th of March, 1957 in front of an enthused crowd when they declared the independence of their country. Its name would change from Gold Coast to Ghana, the name of one of the oldest West African empires. Ghana is free for ever, Nkrumah told his people.

When Ghana gained independence, the public mood was marked by exuberance and hope for immediate and substantial change. And the leadership lived up to the expectations of their people: at least this is the general opinion. After the proclamation of independence, Nkrumah instituted a voluntarist and ambitious policy, aimed at enabling Ghana to evolve, and break away from past limitations. In particular, he wanted to develop Ghana's agriculture so that she would not depend anymore on cocoa alone, which when prices fell, would put the country in a delicate situation. He also wanted to reduce Ghana's dependence in relation to foreign manufactured items, and change his country's role from the sole role of supplier of raw materials. He built roads, hospitals, a university and several industrial projects, including a very ambitious hydroelectric dam on the River Volta.

The base for a healthy take-off, and of the State of Ghana according to the wishes of the people was laid.

Contrasting in the case of *La République du Cameroun* three years later, we had a spoiler. So-called independence was preceded by French intriguing, internal betrayals, French heavy-handedness with nationalists, and selective liquidation of militants for unification and genuine independence and the political decision to decapitate the most important independence movement, the *Union des Populations du Cameroun (U.P.C.)*. Ruben Um Nyobe,[1] the Secretary General of the *U.P.C.*, was *assassinated* by the French colonial army on 13th September, 1958. Less than one year and a half after, the French awarded formal political *independence* to *La République du Cameroun*. Ruben Um Nyobe had to be *slain* before Cameroon would be awarded independence![2]

When Ruben Um Nyobe invited all Cameroonians to be part of the fight for freedom he said that: First due to slavery, and then colonialism, the African continent suffered so much violence inflicted on it by other peoples. Slave dealers did not consider Africans as human beings. Colonialists thought that Africans needed to be civilised and were incapable of organising their lives. In colonialism, their land and natural resources were exploited and the profits carted away. The fight for independence was a first step towards an affirmation of their being as humans and then a reaffirmation of their identity as peoples with the right to be in charge of their own affairs. This was the objective of the first movements for independence.

This dissertation is on the recent history of Cameroon of the years leading to independence: the question we try to answer relates to the predilection to resort to authoritarian ways in the way issues are handled in the *decolonised* Cameroon. Most of our sources are secondary: video documentaries on the recent history of Cameroon, archived video recordings of paper presentations by scholars, archived audio and televised panel discussions, and published works by historians. Some data, not much, are primary data, on events of police and paramilitary action in cities, and on university campuses of which we were eye witness or of falsifiable live video recordings circulated by means of the Internet social networks. We used an analytical tool which is familiar to interpretative social scientists, namely, the ideal-type proposed by Vico, Montesquieu, and Max Weber. The cardinal concepts of our ideal-type are *brutality* in politics, frequent non-authorisation of public meetings, harassing of political entities which are not in sympathy with the party and government in power, use of cunning, orders of arrests decided outside of procedures of the law, state-advised and initiated actions of violence perpetrated by state agents and blamed on agitators to make wanton action of state forces in charge of maintaining law and order seem necessary, impressive and frequent assault paramilitary presences in city centres especially in Yaoundé, police and paramilitary options [raids, and beating up of people by supposed *forces* of defence and security acting as forces for the maintenance of law and order (policemen)], and blunt show of power and use of lethal force. The constructs in the manner in which they are related to one another amount to an artifice which is entertained and set in motion to respond to every single event in the polity which might lead to social movements.

Translations of texts from French into English were done by the author.

---

[1] The Secretary General of the *U.P.C.*; his people called him "*podol lǫŋ*; the "*Mpodol*" – the Basaa term for "the people's spokesman."
[2] *Il fallait tuer Ruben Um Nyobe pour accorder l'Indépendance au Cameroun.*

CHAPTER ONE
GENERAL CONSIDERATIONS

After its defeat in Indochina and in Algeria, regarding French-controlled territories of Africa, the basic concern for the Republic of France was the perpetuation of its domination over African peoples. Because they thought that it was bad for the French economy to give independence to the mandated territory under the leadership of the *U.P.C.* who sought the *re*-unification of the two then existing Cameroons [the Northern and Southern British Cameroons under British control as part of Nigeria, and French-controlled Cameroon], and genuine independence, the French created scaremonger political formations who drew their membership from the colonial administration they could manipulate against the proposed enterprise of conscientisation of the masses being undertaken by the *U.P.C..*

To prepare for the formal granting of the *independence* they were going to give to Cameroon, on 25th May, 1955, the French created an incident in Douala when the *U.P.C.* requested for crucial elections so that the comparative weights of the political formations within Cameroon could be seen. Knowing the facts about the formations they were sponsoring, the French instigated violence and set out to deal with it, so as to suggest to international opinion [the UN] that in such conditions, normal elections could not be organised and that peace should first be restored. Actually, it was scheming, thought out, to get rid of a major nationalist movement to whom they would not hand an independent Cameroon. The movement was banned. The leadership of the *U.P.C.* was *tracked* to every single individual: its leaders were judicially harassed, its meetings were broken, homes of known and supposed militants were raided, and ordinary militants were arrested, beaten up and tortured. In this, the colonial administration was "ably assisted by the Catholic Church, which launched its own anti-communist crusade against the *UPC.*"[1] There were massive movements of populations, including several *U.P.C* leaders, across the western border into British Southern Cameroons. Pursuing French forces dispatched death squads to kill *U.P.C.* elements in Kumba or in Bamenda.

Pierre Messmer, the French High Commissioner for French Cameroon (1956-1958) who replaced Rolland Pré, proposed internal autonomy for Cameroon to be preceded by elections (the first ever) in 1956 to choose representatives for a local assembly which would handle ordinary matters. The *U.P.C.* though with reservations, welcomed the idea of elections and prepared to take part in them but stumbled against French intriguing and obstruction: the French would not lift the ban on the *U.P.C.*

Could the French be trusted to organise fair elections in Cameroon? The UN would be at the side of the issue and *U.P.C.*'s main card against French continued suzerainty, [unification before independence] would become secondary. Out frustration the movement launched a campaign for civil disobedience. The peoples of French Cameroon would not participate in elections. The French decided to corrupt its leader to stand alone for elections. The leadership of French Cameroon to whom the management of the affairs of the state would be given at decolonisation, we said, was the choice of the French. When their position on the big questions of the moment [unification of French Cameroon and English Cameroon and *independence*] were considered, it turned out that they were what we have termed mock nationalists. For these so-called leaders of the anti-colonial struggle, the main issue was the hope that they would convert their leadership

---

[1]Augusta_Conchiglia_Ghosts of Kamerun_NHR 77_September-October 2012.Pdf. p. 7.

positions into individual mobility. Political office was seen as a path away from poverty.[2] Concerned about the moment of the issues at stake, and true to the stated positions of the movement he led, the *mpodol* would not come under this category. He would not be bribed.

On the eve of elections, two candidates who had the support of the French, lost their lives through some action supposed by the French to be the action of *U.P.C.* hardliners. The *U.P.C.* was accused of being responsible for the violence; the French called the situation which arose an insurrection, and the movement and its militants were *outlawed*. The scheduled election despite the *U.P.C.* largely heeded call to the Cameroonian people not to turn out for elections, still took place. A state of exception was declared. Apparently the French had anticipated something like this.

We are in the middle of the Cold War [between the Western and the Eastern blocs]: the French alerted the Western bloc of the risk of its territories slipping into the communist bloc. For those in power in France, there was no question of foregoing French grandeur, power and the riches she got from her empire. Nasser, Tito, Nehru on the one hand and Moscow, and China on the other hand worsened this fear. The defeat inflicted by the Vietcong[3] [Indochina] guerillas was a sort of humiliation of the French Army. Every movement which challenged its supremacy was classified in the bloc of communists. Indochina would serve as a lesson: the French army theorised a new war – the so-called revolutionary war at the time when the first incidents broke out in Algeria. French soldiers who had been to Indochina were sent to Algeria to apply the new doctrine of psychological war. Its targets were civilians. Behind every single man it was supposed, was hidden a potential enemy. Pierre Messmer would with some candour volunteer that: *"Nous avions tous, surtout ceux qui avaient été en Indochine, réfléchi aux dispositifs, et nous en savions beaucoup."*[4] He immediately called for reinforcing troops of the French colonial army in Congo Brazzaville and took the repression of the *U.P.C.* movement to a higher level this time with no plan to stop before the complete physical elimination of every single militant including the *mpodol*. He ordered the *extermination* of the peoples of the Sanaga-Maritime Region!

> « *Bombardement, tortures, exécution extrajudiciaire, levée des milices, guerre psychologique, regroupement forcés de populations... Les méthodes employées sont celles qui avaient cours au même moment pendant la guerre d'Algérie. Leur emploi s'est poursuivi de longues années, après l'indépendance du Cameroun [...]».*[5]

Douala and environing towns and the countryside of Basaaland where the leadership of the *U.P.C.* sought refuge, were flooded with paramilitary forces and troops of the French colonial army, militia recruited from among its marionette political formations from areas especially of the north of the territory where *U.P.C.* conscientisation activity was less successful,[6] and

---

[2]Specifically referring to politicians of the former British Southern Cameroons, on the issue of unification after the referendum of 1961, Solomon Muna and John Ngu Foncha in their relations with the Ahmadou Ahidjo regime for different reasons have been cited in this category.

[3]The anti-colonial movement against French colonial rule in North Vietnam.

[4]We all, especially those who had been to Indochina, thought over on the device, and we knew a lot.

[5]Bombing, tortures, extrajudicial killings, recruiting of militias, psychological warfare, forced regrouping of populations... The methods were those which were being used at the same time in the war in Algeria. Their use continued several years after independence for French Cameroon. Manuel Domergue, Thomas Deltombe, Jacob Tatsitsa in *Kamerun ! Une guerre cachée aux origines de la Francafrique* (1948 1971).

[6]Fulani chiefdoms of the north were quite unreceptive to *U.P.C.* education of the masses: the achievement of independence, for its implication of democratisation, would undermine their own [colonial] domination over non-Islamised populations. As a matter of fact the north of Cameroon, which has a majority of Muslim populations identified the Christian populations of the south with the *U.P.C.* and thus with the demand for independence. It has

mercenaries and assorted bounty hunters. The colonial army used armoured tanks, automatic weapons, helicopter gunships and deadly chemical fire bombs and sprays against a handful of militants who in defense had only clubs, machetes and firearms for the hunting of game. *The marching order was: kill, kill everyone and everything.* It was a devastation and slaughter: there was indiscriminate killing – unarmed men, women, children, old men, livestock were slaughtered. Even forests were burned and habitation destroyed by fire. Dogs and flesh-eating birds were given great feasts for several months. *Entire villages were burned and the inhabitants all killed.*

Between February and March 1960, several Bamiléké villages were burnt down and bulldozed: 116 classrooms, 3 hospitals, 46 dispensaries, 12 agricultural stations, 40 bridges were destroyed. No stock has been taken of the destruction of private property, and burnt harvests, nor of the tens of thousands of civilians killed. To talk of genocide, the Bamiléké people have suffered others between 1955 and 1965. The figures are set at between 800000 and 1000000 people in the *Région des Haut Plateaux* and in towns such as Douala, Yaounde, Sangmelima, Ebolowa and Nkongsamba. To this date, the mere mention of this period to anyone of Bamiléké origin with some memory provokes goose bumps. This premeditated and systematically executed crime of France went on for several years.

It is interesting to consider the dreadfulness with which the repression of the *U.P.C.* movement was undertaken. Commenting the repression by the colonial army, and the death by firing squad of Ernest Ouandié, the President of *La République du Cameroun sous Maquis*, an active military commander at the time would scoff at accusations against the government installed by France that Ouandié was assassinated, and extol, with impudence, the method of *regroupement* used by the colonial army he served. "It is said that 156 small villages in the Basaa region were razed in 1960-1961 on the pretext of 'regrouping' the inhabitants..." A helicopter pilot who was in the French army in Cameroun at the time, Marx Barthec, wrote in a book he published in the 1980s, that, in two years – 1962-1964 – the army in a systematic scheme, ravaged Bamileke land from the South to the North. Between 300,000 and 400,000 people were killed. Entire villages were razed from existence, that is, after the passage of the army, nothing was left.

There were massacres, summary executions, even hostages executed."[7] The method of *regroupement* was that, peasants in the forests were forcefully moved [frightened away from their homes] and confined in specific parts of the territory as it is suggested in the concept of *reserved forests* [their houses were razed and crops destroyed]. *Outside of the camps would be found the wild beast and the criminal,*[8] French propaganda said, and at any time, anyone – men, women, children, fauna and *flora* which could or sometimes seemed to move – who was not within the reserved zones [*zones de pacification in the Sanaga-Maritime*][9] was tracked and killed. In the forest, the Secretary General of the *U.P.C.*, the *mpodol*, had installed a parallel government. The population in the countryside continued to run away from the army to live in the territory known to be free. One third of the south of the territory was thus free.

---

been suggested that for them, political emancipation preached by the *U.P.C.* was an avenue to southern [Christian in the majority] domination and would have preferred [encouraged by the French] to have their region annexed to their neighbours [Chad and Ubangi-Shari] under French administration.

[7]Submission credited to M. Charles Van de Lanoitte in Joseph, Richard (Ed.) (1978). *Gaullist Africa: Cameroon under Ahmadou Ahidjo.* Enugu: Fourth Dimension Publishers. P. 96.

[8]Psychological war as had been carried out before in Indochina and in Algeria.

[9]A year-long suspension of colonial legality to deal with opponents who in many cases were armed with little more than machetes and clubs.

Did those Cameroonians who served in the colonial army have any political education and know what the term "colonialism" stands for? We wonder. Let us say that they were mere foot soldiers.

A common view relates the European initiative to colonise the world as part of a "civilising mission." The French government portrayed their colonial enterprise as *"rayonnement,"* lighting the way for others (Cole and Raymond, 2006: 158-159). In the colonies, subjects were taught that they were colonised for their own good and that their societies would advance as a result. In Britain, citizens were encouraged to take up *the white man's burden* of bringing civilisation to the *savage.* In the implicit discourse of the colonialists, Africans in their service could not be anything more than mere flesh animated from without for action towards specified objectives of their masters.

Should one expect more brains among foot soldiers when their political leaders [so-called intellectual] commanders would accept to be bribed and to be paraded as lovers of the colonial regime who are against decolonisation and independence, and later would actually and with no qualms, *maintain* in place, *the system* of their masters of yesterday?

But for a Cameroonian who became a senior member of the colonial army to extol those methods of the French and have no qualms regarding his role in the massacres and desolation that they caused [mass and lasting trauma, hopelessness and ruin of a country] so many years after those episodes, this is a curiosity. As a foot soldier at the time of the atrocities, it may be entertained that he could have been relatively ignorant and absolvable of personal responsibility. But he became a senior member of that army! It is of singular interest to say the least, that he is still not *touched in his feelings* by the methods and the extent of the killings. Even the French have since admitted that they struck too hard, and with other methods they could have obtained better results, and at a lower price.[10] To an enquiring journalist who interviewed him on the events of repression during the period of decolonisation and after, he would respond [chest pounding]: *"Oui oui! C'est mon armée, qui coupait la tête des maquisards."*[11] Or, should we not hail the man for his ability to appreciate complexities of political science such as domains of nationalism? Yea! Nationalism is of complexities for any a foot soldier of colonial Africa, and for sure for most of them in the ranks even to this date. The foot soldier kills or gets killed, period!

The French are very informed on difficult times of the past and bad things which have happened to them in their history. And they want everyone to know. Their attitude is rather different when it is other people who want their own past to be well-known and want anyone to talk about it. Africans, who do not want their past of slavery and colonial domination to be forgotten, are accused of victimisation; they should leave all that; they are just minutiae [trivia]. Africans are enjoined to forget. Colonial wars are very little known: books or fiction which deal with the wars of Indochina and Algeria, are few and little read. There seem to be a complete blackout on what happened in Madagascar in 1947 and especially in Cameroon from 1955 to 1971. French policies regarding these issues is characterised by disinformation, distortion and especially deliberate oversight. Pierre Messmer, the French High Commissioner who supervised the massacres in the UN-Cameroon during the period of 1956-1958, when asked [about fifty years later] whether he had heard of the use of napalm [a chemical weapon] in the bush war in French Cameroon, he accepted, but quickly added, *"c'est pas important,"* [it is a detail, it is not relevant].

---

[10] *Main basse sur le Cameroun* published by François Maspero in 1972.

[11] "Yea! It is my army which chopped off the heads of insurgents." Submission volunteered to M. Domergue by Pierre Semengué when he was assembling material for a book, *Kamerun! Histoire d'une guerre cachée* he co-wrote with J. Tatsitsa and T. Deltombe.

Figure 1. French troops in Cameroon pose for show with their trophies

"The use of collective punishment and summary executions became systematic; 'disappearances' multiplied, while captured fighters or their relatives were repeatedly tortured to extract information."[13] When the forces of the colonial army arrested fugitives in the forest, [to kill them, their heads were cut off and for the effect, cut off heads were frequently taken to the market place] ... or *were the necks blown off, were the heads cut off after the death of the victims*?

France denies that such things happened. Until recently, the denial was only implicit – implied by French censorship of news reports in news papers and published works.

But in 2009, invited to Cameroon for the yearly 20th May celebration, the French Prime Minister, François Fillon, gave a press conference and a female journalist of a local television asked him what France was going to do with regard to victims of a war in which nationalist leaders were assassinated by the French army. Textually, François Fillon responded: "I deny that French forces participated in assassinations. All that is a pure lie."[14]

This response, coming from a French Prime Minister, was beyond belief to say the least, to many a political observer. This was a man who was born in 1954, who has done studies in journalism and in law, who once was an assistant in the French National Assembly before a career in politics which led him to become Minister for Higher Education and Research, and to become the Prime Minister of France. Perhaps he had never heard a single word of this history. So, for him it was a fabrication. And yet it is of the recent history of his own country! Could he have

---

[12]Submission volunteered to M. Domergue by Pierre Semengué.

[13]Source: Augusta_Conchiglia_Ghosts of Kamerun_NHR 77_September-October 2012.Pdf. Review of Thomas Deltombe, Manuel Domergue and Jacob Tatsitsa, *Kamerun! Une guerre cachée aux origines de la Françafrique, 1948–1971*. La Découverte: Paris 2011.

[14]*En 2009, invité au Cameroun pour la fête du 20 mai le Premier Ministre français François Fillon tient une conférence de presse à Yaoundé, et une journaliste d'une télévision locale lui demande ce que la France compte faire à l'égard des victimes d'une guère où des leaders nationalistes ont été assassiné par l'armée française. François Fillon répond textuellement «Je dénie absolument que des forces françaises aient participé, en quoi que ce soit, à des assassinats au Cameroun. Tout cela, c'est de la pure invention!»* Source: Guerre au Cameroun_histoire d'une censure obstinée et persistante - ODILE TOBNER (www search).

lied as part of a scheme? Did he really not know? We can only speculate on what is the case. This caused an uproar in Cameroon, but in France it was a silence of silence in silence.

For the French in France, and also in Cameroon ruled by *Cameroonians* [governors decided by France], the war in Cameroon did not take place. Officially, there are no ceremonies, no commemorations. In 2008, when some students of a certain association, [*Association pour la Défense des Droits des Etudiants du Cameroun*], a small group of perhaps about ten, went to Eseka, to have a moment of recollection at the tomb of Ruben Um Nyobe on the fiftieth anniversary of his *assassination*, they were accosted by the police and taken to the District Officer and were asked what they wanted to do. It cannot be said that anything is being done in Cameroon – about ten students, this created a political problem when they tried to get to the tomb of Ruben Um Nyobe. Felix Rolland Moumié was the President of the *U.P.C.* He was killed by poisoning: a French agent [posing as a journalist] secretly put poison in his drink while he was in Switzerland to negotiate for arms needed by *U.P.C.* militants to defend themselves against slaughter by the French Army. This was in 1960. His remains have disappeared in the Republic of Guinea where he was buried; there is no tomb anymore in Conakry. There was an attempt to cause the tomb of Ernest Ouandié – the last of the leaders of the *U.P.C.* in insurgency – to disappear. In 1972 Mongo Beti[15] had the misfortune to write a book, *Main basse sur le Cameroun* in which he gave a synopsis of the history of French disinformation on the war up to the acme of misrepresentation in the report of headlines of the newspaper, *Le Monde*, on the trial of Ernest Ouandié, who gave himself up in 1970, condemned after something like a trial in a court, to death and executed in January 1971. This book was immediately banned by decree of the French Minister of Interior. After the book, French police went for the author and sought to rescind his French nationality. He would defeat the French State in court but he was definitively black listed by pseudo-cultural media which were completely devoted to the *official French version* on events on the former colonies. The book would be read only in secret by a small number of Cameroonians who learn the bloody history of their country.

Colonial wars were wars of hatred, wars of extermination; colonial peoples were supposed to be sub-humans, to be eliminated. According to the French and according to the personnel they installed as the "governors" of Cameroon [some of whom are still around and in affairs], there were no assassinations, there were no mass killings in French Cameroon.

The extermination of the nationalists was *a five on five* military success and was sealed by a censorship which suppressed the memory of the event – a *perfect crime* as some would qualify it.

France finally acknowledges the occurrence of these sad events : « *C'est vrai qu'il y a eu des épisodes tragique dans l'histoire. Il y a eu une répression dans la Sanaga-Maritime et en pays Bamiléké* [...] » a French president, François Hollande, declared in Yaounde on 3rd July, 2015.

The French gave internal autonomy to French Cameroon in 1958, after making mock nationalists of the *État sous tutelle* sign agreements with them in practically all domains of life in the territory: economy, finance, education, and culture. For leadership, they installed the very *opponents* of unification and independence in the person of [André-Marie Mbida and then Ahmadou Ahidjo] and his government and the UN territory under French tutelage was granted political *independence* in 1960[16] and continued repression against *U.P.C.*, and assassination of its militants for another ten to twelve years.

---

[15]Pen name for Allexandre Biyidi.

[16]France supported French Cameroon to become a member state of the UN on 20th September 1960, whilst British Cameroons continued to remain as a trust territory.

After independence in 1960, they got the emergent government to sign a treaty that mentioned that the territory was to cede all powers of government to France and that it could not administer its affairs independently without prior French approval. The new republic would exploit any natural resource only if it was clear that the French were not interested in its exploitation and they would still be present through their army, the activities of their firms and as sorts of technical advisers in the government. Referring to these agreements a French Cameroonian expert in international law[17] used the term *"reconduction du système colonial sous forme de contrat."*[18] Was this independence?

The group of natives educated by the French to staff the colonial economy, sought its own benefit. Theorising on the posture of such leadership Frantz Fanon says the emergent *middle class* clamoured to fill the privileged posts of the occupying colonial power after independence not to lead the nation into development, but to secure profits and government concessions and be bosses. A tendency to cling to political office quickly arose. It would not be far-fetched to suppose that the so called independent Cameroon is more *a land* of *administered* peoples than a self-governing and an *independent* country.

---

[17]Abel Eyinga.

[18]La Republique du Cameroun was granted conditional Independence by France on 1st January 1960, on terms that it first executed a "Co-operation Agreement" with Trustee France on 26th December 1959 by literally yielding all operating power over the Trust Territory to France, its Trust Administrator: money, foreign affairs, defense and strategic raw materials would remain under French control.

CHAPTER TWO
POLITICAL DEVELOPMENT AND THE STRUGGLE FOR INDEPENDENCE

Just before the World War II, in the face of German clamouring to regain its territories of before World War I, the French thought that they had to prepare Africans, especially Cameroonians, who among them were many who still had strong links with the former colonial power – it was not so long since Germany was ousted – sympathisers with even circles of friends in some towns who used to meet to dink together and speak German. For the sake of prudence, it was thought that the population was to be prepared against German propaganda.

On the instigation of the Governor General Richard Bruno *JeuCaFra*,[1] an officious propaganda tool whose aim was to show that the people of Cameroon were not in favour of being *re*-united with Nazi Germany, was formed with Soppo Priso as leader. It was also an opportunity for the French to further ensure their authority on this territory which had a special status since it was not a colony like others but conferred by the League of Nations to Britain and France after the defeat of Germany in 1918. Ruben Um Nyobe like other learned young Cameroonians at the time, joined *JeuCaFra* in 1939. For Ruben Um Nyobe however, this movement was of interest to them not for the reasons of the colonialists. In this regard, he wrote:

> *Pour nous, il se présentait comme la meilleure occasion d'affirmer publiquement que nous étions pour la liberté et contre le totalitarisme et par conséquent nous manifestions notre attachement à la France contre le retour sous une administration allemande Hitlérienne. Mais cela ne signifiait pas pour nous, que nous demandions à devenir colonie française comme l'affirmait abusivement Monsieur Soppo Priso.*[2]

In the early stage of the War, Germany occupied France without a fight. General Charles de Gaulle went to Brazzaville in 1940 and launched a call for African territories under French control to support *Free* France and the call was largely adhered to by Africans. In tens of thousands, they went to Europe to support French effort.

After the Second World War, when servicemen returned from that war, things were bound to evolve. The awareness of servicemen had evolved as a result of exposure: at the war they were *brothers in arms* with French men; they had seen their weaknesses, lived their doubts, their fears and other events of everyday life. Ordinarily, for most of them, they used to think that White people were some sort of super beings. Not anymore. They were also aware of their contribution to the saving of France and that France owed them acknowledgement.

Intellectuals too, nursed the hope that the collaboration in the war, the support of their people to enable the French to triumph over Nazism would lead the French to some humility, but especially, to widen their rights and to give then some liberty. If they had fought for the French to enable them regain their freedom, it was logical that the French accord to them their autonomy. The French were conscious that in the face of the acquired awareness among the indigenes, they had to make concessions.

---

[1] *Jeunesse Camerounaise Française.*

[2] For us it was the best opportunity to publicly affirm that we were for freedom, against totalitarianism and as a consequence, we were manifesting our attachment to France against returning to German administration under Hitler. This did not however mean that we were requesting to become a French colony as Soppo Priso was abusively affirming.

On 30th July, 1944, General de Gaulle went to Brazzaville (then the capital of *Afrique Equatoriale Française*) to express French gratitude to Africans for the role they played in the Second World War. It was a great moment for Africans. General de Gaulle's visit however, did not lead to an end of discrimination and social injustice (forced labour nor of the *régime d'indigénat*[3]). He excluded the prospects of autonomy and evolution outside the French empire, but he, in passing, alluded to the participation of natives in the management of their own affairs. The General also evoked the possibility of natives acting and organising themselves freely. The first decree of the provisional government of France under De Gaulle would authorise the formation of Trade Unions.

On social and related issues, the French were willing to improve the conditions of the colonised. Daily life was a really bad case of disdain for a huge part of the masses. The colonial regime would be softened:

> Forced labour was abolished [in the regime of forced labour, natives could be arbitrarily taken away once and for ever, from their homes and families – up-rooted – and made to work with neither pay nor concern for their work condition and welfare.

> The *régime d'indigénat* was also abolished.

> These concessions were granted to stave off impending general revolts.

Demands for separation from France, quitting the empire, however, were out of the question. Moukoko Priso relates a submission of one of his teachers at the time as follows: *C'était... bon, Négros, vous n'êtes bons à rien, vous ne pouvez rein faire de bon etc. etc. ...vous ne pouvez pas diriger un état moderne.*[4]

A French political party, *le Parti Communiste Français* in September, 1945 made a decision to create study circles in sub-Saharan lands to train militants. Influential intellectuals of the country rushed to belong, first, because these circles enabled them to acquire a systems perspective and to interpret and fight the economic and political aspects of colonialism, and then, it gave them the first opportunity to meet White people and to work with them as equals. These circles had different names. In Yaoundé, a certain Gaston Donnat [militant of the French Communist Party] created a study circle called the *Cercle d'Études Marxiste* and after, the *Cercle d'Etudes Sociale*. Ruben Um Nyobe and his friend Jacques Ngom attended these circles with assiduity. It is in the *Cercle d'Etudes Sociale* that they learned concepts of politics and techniques of militants

To crystallise the articulation Ruben Um Nyobe made between trade union activism and political struggle, he, on 28th July 1944, formed the *Union des Syndicats Conféderés du Cameroun.*[5]

Two events were to quicken the political evolution of Cameroon.

First there was the commemoration of those who fell in battle [World War II] on the 1st November 1944. The colonialists applauded and participated. It was great joy, great fraternity. Then about six months later, the call of the *Union des Syndicats Conféderés du Cameroun*: with coffins in display, the movement called for the symbolic burial of Nazism, of racism and of colonialism. The French [Europeans] were shocked, *scandalised*. They thought that so much of rights given to natives to form associations made their own position frail. To compare with their condition before and during the war, things were getting worse for them. They reacted by

---

[3]In *régime d'indigénat*, there was a legal system for the indigenes and another legal system for the colonial settlers.
[4]It was... good, Negros, you are good at nothing, you cannot do anything good, etc. etc. ... you cannot manage a modern state. Submission credited to Moukoko Priso.
[5] Gaston Donnat was the first Secretary General.

forming their own association, *l'Association des Colons du Cameroun* (*ASCOCAM*) to try to stop social demands – in reaction against French concessions in favour of Cameroonians.

To the movement's call for the burial of Nazism, colonialism and racism, the colonial administration responded with repression. The militants are radicalised. In September 1945 workers of the railway corporation went on a strike for salaries and the strike would spread to all sectors. The colonial administration shot at manifesting crowds and this led to riots and deaths of scores of persons. The French militants in the *Union des Syndicats Conféderés du Cameroun* including its Secretary General were expelled and sent back to France: in the thinking of the French, Cameroonians were incapable of thinking. Depriving them of the white people among them, they would be lost.

Ruben Um Nyobe became Secretary General of the movement.

Increased confrontations with the white organisation led Ruben Um Nyobe and his colleagues to think that another organisation should be formed in which they would consider distinctively political questions. The *U.P.C.* was formed and authorised as a political movement on 10th April 1948 and Ruben Um Nyobe was plebiscited to become its Secretary General in November, 1948.

When the Secretary General of the *U.P.C.* went to New York in 1952 after a long battle with Paris for a visa, which he finally obtained with the help of Jean-Paul Sartre, he made the case for independence against the Cameroonian placement sent by Paris, such as Douala Manga Bell. He told the General Assembly of the UN Organisation (UNO) that his people had mandated him to put forth to the international community three items:

> *L'UPC à demandé intervenir sur trois questions: La réunification immédiate du Cameroun; La constitution d'un conseil de gouvernement et d'une assemblée avec des pouvoirs législatifs; et enfin, la fixation d'un délai pour l'octroi de l'indépendance au peuple camerounais.*

Its request to the international community was that the Cameroons [the British administered component and the French-administered component] were to be *united*, a governing council and an assembly with law-making powers constituted, and a timeline of events towards independence given. Apparently this was a normal request; the two entities used to be one and for viability, the bigger the country at independence, the better. Actually, the *U.P.C.* had been incensed by French non-wish to grant independence to French colonies. The *U.P.C*'s request for *re*-unification was its reminder to the international community that Cameroon was *not* a French colony. Cameroon was a UN-trusted territory administered under French and British tutelage. The political development of the territory was the concern of the UN: it was incumbent on the UN and not on the French or on the British to grant independence to Cameroon. On this reminder, the French tried to change the status of the territory under Trusteeship but stumbled against *U.P.C.* mass education: whence the decision and scheme to implement their own agenda.

In the same year and in the following year (1952 and 1953), the UN adopted a resolution pressing the French to move towards autonomy. Reluctant to grant independence to peoples under their domination, the French proposed to transform their African colonies into *collectivités territoriales* of France overseas. In the preamble of the constitution of the *République de France* during the colonial era it was stated that: *La France forme avec les peuples d'outremer, une union fondée sur l'égalité des droits et devoirs sans distinction de race ou de religion.*[6] However,

---

[6]With the peoples overseas, France was a union based on equality in rights and duties without distinctions of race and religion.

the political order in what the French were proposing was manifestly, biased: in terms of political representation in the legislative component that would be put in place, a double college, the legislative body would comprise of councillors in the proportions of one for every 250 French settlers, and one for every 166000 Cameroonians. A stark parallel existed already in South Africa. Alerted by the action of the *U.P.C.* which made its militants aware that Cameroon was *not* a French colony, and so would not be involved in the scheme the French proposed, the French undertook to *create* Cameroonians who would speak for *Cameroonians* who *wanted* the UN-Trusted territory of Cameroon to become a French colony and a certain Duala chief, Manga Bell was paraded at the UN Organisation to tell the world that *Cameroonians loved France and demanded that the UN-Trusted territory of Cameroon become a French colony.*

This probably was a partial explanation of *U.P.C.*'s insistence on the *re*unification of the two Cameroons *before* independence. In this light it would have been awkward to lump Cameroon within the so-called *collectivités territoriales* of France overseas. Some have suggested that this was the single idea which led the French to decide and order the elimination of its leadership and the assassination of the *mpodol.*

U.P.C. action on political conscientisation had been in process since the creation of the movement in 1948. Its leadership had thought out explicit plans in respect to political governance upon independence. Already, in practice, the mode of organisation within the *U.P.C.* itself and the effectiveness which characterised its masses education enterprise were indicative of the deliberateness with which it prepared for independence. Our movement, arising from the people, nothing valid and constructive would be attained if we act from above as it is the case in the colonies: the role of committees at the base, is to build from the bottom, the *mpodol* would ceaselessly repeat.

Specifically, the *U.P.C.* was sponsoring and supervising the training of a sizable personnel to man the government when the country would be accorded independence. As a matter of fact, at the time when its activities were banned and its militants outlawed, it had more knowledgeable people among its following for this event within and out of Cameroon than the French among the scaremonger of political formations they sponsored within Cameroon. It was very advanced in the preparation of the territory for self rule and independence.

In the single person of the *mpodol*, the Secretary General, it has been acknowledged, was extraordinary as an organiser and as a masses educator. He was a remarkable polyglot" being able to express himself with the same readiness in Basaa, Ewondo, Bulu, Pidgin English, and in French. He travelled tirelessly across the country, "from village to village, on train, by foot, by tuck," seeking to persuade his compatriots. He eschewed abstract discourse of theories of liberation and independence. The spotlight of his public interventions were on the daily concerns of the people of the countryside and of urban areas regarding, the price of cocoa, the price of salt, the prices of items imported from France, increasing unemployment, the insufficiency of hospitals and the spotted disdain of the colonial administrators towards Cameroonians. Even his enemies had to concede his "honesty and moral rigour": internal police reports describe him as "a politician who sees clearly and far" and "a man of merit."

The colonial regime, by means of disinformation led the colonised to believe that he was inferior. The *U.P.C*'s counter measure was, education and political training. The *mpodol* taught *U.P.C.* masses that Cameroon belonged to Cameroonians; Cameroonians should be aware of who they are as humans; at all, that they are to no degree, *lesser humans* than the French who at that time, dominated in their land.

The struggle of the *U.P.C.* was for the attainment of the actualisation of two things: colonial domination and slavery had debased the African. Independence would restore to the Cameroonian this loss of dignity through an affirmation of his identity. The attainment of independence meant that Cameroon would be governed by Cameroonians for Cameroonians.

The *mpodol* warned against independence which might not be genuine. Actually, he was warning against what was to come, namely, the neo-colonial regime. La République du Cameroun as we have it today is the pure type of the very independent republic that the *mpodol* warned against in his conscientisation exhortations of the peoples of Cameroon – the neo-colonial republic *par excellence*. Independence was genuine only if in reality, it meant economic and social emancipation. With Ruben Um Nyobe, the workers were made aware of their rights. We are in 1950. To mobilise Cameroonian workers, Ruben Um Nyobe had this lesson for them. The capitalist he affirms, has the support of the colonial administration and this administration can carry out its policy of oppression in our land only by using economic weapons and technical means which on the main are in the possession of enterprises. The *U.P.C.* thinks, and trade union militants are also of the opinion, that, economic emancipation of our populations is impossible without the political victories necessary for economic, social and cultural progress.

As with many other countries before colonisation, Cameroon is characterised by ethnic, cultural and religious diversity. The coloniser made of this fact an instrument of division by playing off ethnic groups against ethnic groups, and religious groups against religious groups – causing division so that it would reign. It occurred that the movement the *mpodol* led was accused of tribalism. In response, it is in record that the *mpodol* alluded to the concept of the nation which is not shy to affirm its cultural plurality.

Ruben Um Nyobe is one of those African leaders who specifically thought out the construction of a nation. The leader of the *U.P.C.* proposed a conception of the nation as having to be united without being unique. He made a distinction between the unity of a nation and cultural oneness. He highlighted the link between political unity of a nation and the cultural diversity of its peoples and recoiled against the idea that the nation, under the pretext of unity may oppress or deny the rights of minorities.

For the *mpodol*, it did not suffice to unite the two parts of the territory divided by colonialism for there to be a nation. Cameroonians were to attain a sharp awareness of their culture which would enable a projection of their complete anchorage in their culture, but at the same time, in their resistance against the coloniser, people of different tribes, people of different religions which in history had been engaged in confrontation, faced the same danger of death ... of survival and were in the same fight. Awareness of this would lead to a process of transcendence of the tribe, not with the objective of doing away with or looking on the tribe with disdain, but the process would usher unto a broader thing, on to a nation on the condition that that nation not turn out to be a negation of diversity. The fact of the tribe was not derogatory but had a historical meaningfulness. The tribe corresponded to a need at some stage of the history of the people. Tribes could be instrumentalised – but this was not sufficient reason to undertake a nationwide detribalisation.

Eschewing tribal bias Um Nyobe had this to say:
> "*Je ne peux accepter en l'état, une prise du pouvoir dans les seuls soucis de protéger les intérêts du colon tout en trahissant, le pacte patriotique et républicain qui lie tous les fils de notre cher pays ceci par la dissolution pure et simple du nationalisme. Le*

The people should not be fooled, the *mpodol* intimated: he enjoined the people not to be forgetful of the fact that there had been an intrusion, that of colonialism. His position was that, the people were to revisit the values of their cultures to reaffirm their cultural roots. On the question of freedom for Cameroon, everyone, whatever his ethnic origin, whatever the religious group with which he identified himself, was in the same fight; emphasis on differences in tribes and in religions while the colonial system lasted, was entertainment [a distraction].

Cameroon was in the category of the oppressed because it is divided; the single objective of the struggle was liberation from the colonial regime; Cameroon would attain victory over its oppressors only as a unified entity, the *mpodol* opined.

In a public submission in May 1955 in front of thousands of persons, in response to the clergy of the Roman Catholic Church [a cardinal had accused Ruben Um Nyobe of anti-White racism] this is what he said:

"*Ce que nous voulons affirmer une fois de plus, c'est que nous sommes contre les colonialistes et leurs hommes de mains, qu'ils soient noirs, blancs ou jaunes, et que nous sommes les alliés de tous les partisans du droit des peuples à disposer d'eux-mêmes, sans considération de couleur. C'est pourquoi catholiques, protestants, musulmans, fétichistes et non-croyants, nous devons nous unir et agir ensemble pour hâter la réunification et l'indépendance du Cameroun.*"[8]

Was the U.P.C. a communist movement? The *mpodol* said that:

"*Les peuples coloniaux ne peuvent faire la politique d'un parti, ni celle d'un état, ni à plus forte raison, celle d'un homme. Les peuples coloniaux feront leur propre politique qui est la libération du peuple du joug colonial et dans leur lutte pour cet objectif si noble, les peuples coloniaux observent et jugent les gouvernements, les partis, les personnes, non sur leurs idéologies et leurs programmes, mais seulement et seulement sur leurs attitudes à l'égard des revendications des peuples de leur pays. Voilà la position de l'Union des Populations du Cameroun au service des peuples du Cameroun.*"

The programmes of political parties, the actions of states, governments and individuals were not of moment as far as the leader of the U.P.C. was concerned. What was important were the attitudes of these entities and of persons within, with regard to the struggle against colonial domination and for freedom.

On violence, the *mpodol* believed that after the defeat of Nazism in Europe, the situation of nations dominating other nations as it was the case of colonialism, was not going to continue. This arose apparently from his analysis of the international situation: the balance of power after the Second World War he thought, was such that colonisation was not going to continue. He

---

[7]For the state, I would not accept power with the sole interest of protecting the interest of the coloniser, betraying patriotic and the republican pact which binds the sons and daughters of our beloved country [...]. Doing this, the Basaa people from whom I arise will enjoy all the privileges of the coloniser but what will become of the other groups? Submission attributed to Um Nyobe in a conversation with Monsignor Thomas Mongo in 1957.

[8]What we want to affirm once more, is that we are against colonialists and their henchmen, be they, black, white or yellow and we are the allies of all partisans of the rights of peoples and nations to be in charge of their own affairs, without consideration of colour. This is the reason why, Catholics, Protestants, Muslims, fetishists and non-believers, we should unite to hasten the reunification and independence of Cameroon.

believed that at the UN, colonised peoples had definite allies who were going to support them in their efforts to put an end to the colonial regime, and indeed they did. Like Gandhi in India before him, Ruben Um Nyobe was of the conviction that his country would attain independence without having to resort to violence and armed struggle. It was at the extreme of moments of colonial action against its militants – arbitrary arrests, institutionalised torture, summary executions, and killing of its leaders – that the movement resorted to armed resistance.

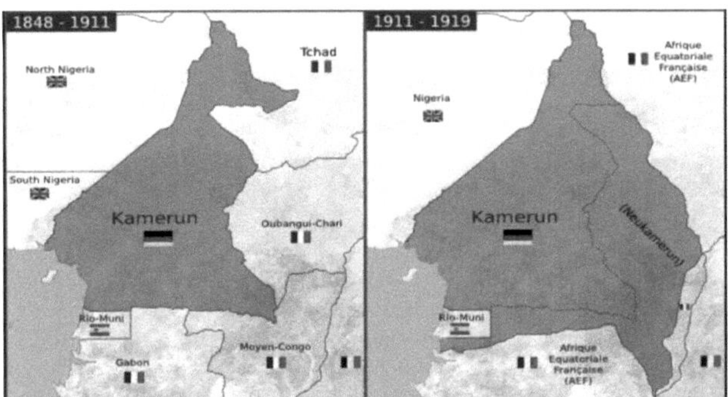

Figure 2.Cameroon as a mandated territory under German control

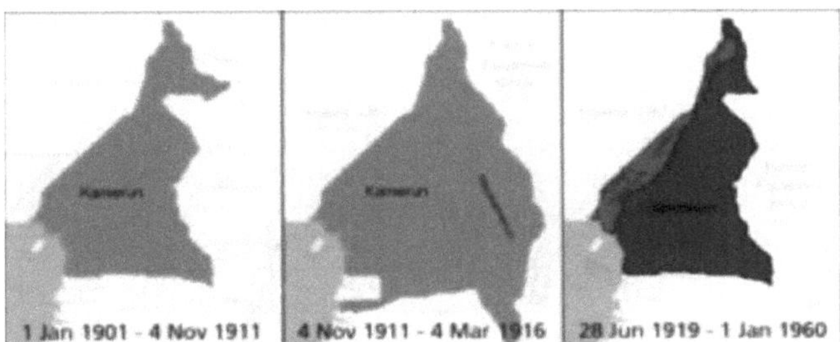

Figure 3.Cameroon as trusted territories partitioned between the French and the British after World War I

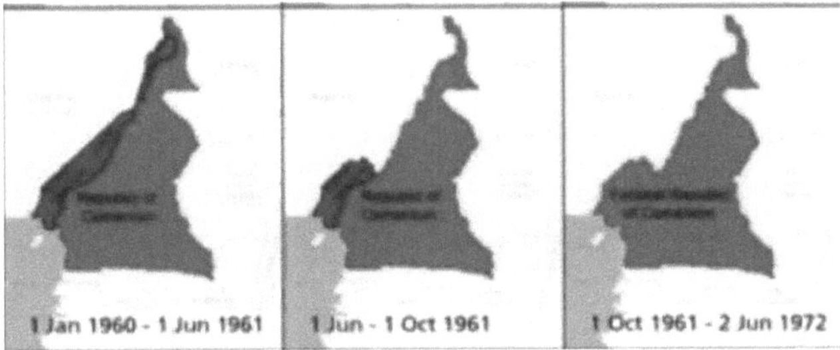

Figure 4. The Cameroons and *La République du Cameroun*

British Cameroons   Southern Cameroons   The Federal Republic of Cameroon
Figure 5. The national flags of British Cameroons and of the Federal Republic of Cameroon

Cameroon entered modern history in 1472 when Portuguese marines sailed up to the estuary of what is now called Wouri River [Gulf of Guinea on the coast of West Africa]. The Portuguese caught numerous small crayfish in the river and, mistaking them for prawns, named the river *Rio dos "Camarões"* – *Camerones* (Spanish), *Kamerun* (German), *Cameroun* (French), and the *Cameroons* (English) – identified the area thereafter and gave the country its present name (LeVine, 1964). From the beginning of the 16th century, the coast of Cameroon was an important source of supply first for Europeans, and later for American slave traders. Britain's attempt to put an end to the West African slave trade during the first half of the 19th century greatly increased British influence in the area. A British mission, the first permanent European settlement in the area, was established at Victoria, at the foot of Mount Cameroon in 1858. Although British interests had an advantage over French and German traders who were active in the region, Britain failed to take advantage of its opportunity to impose its rule on the coast of Cameroon.

In 1884, some firms in Germany signed a treaty with Duala chiefs to exploit the territory in the vicinity of the Wouri Delta [Gulf of Guinea on the coast of West Africa].[1] Shortly after, they surrendered their rights to the state of Germany. With its army Germany extended its control beyond the Delta, establishing a protectorate over what came to be called Kamerun [see maps above]. However, the Treaty was part of a broader European interest in Africa that had been growing through the last quarter of the 19th century. Growing tensions between regions in terms of trade and economic power led to the Berlin West Africa Conference from November 15, 1884 to January 30, 1885. The Conference helped define the jurisdiction of European countries over the regions that they administered, while simultaneously reducing tensions between European superpowers as each raced to establish its own territory. Despite the 1884 agreement, France and Britain concluded at the Anglo-France Conference on August 15, 1914 to jointly attack Cameroon. The defeat of Germany in World War I led to the sanctioned partitioning of the Cameroons, with Britain and France. In 1922, the status of the British and French Cameroons were confirmed as League of Nations mandates.

The territory formally known as German Kamerun was extinguished from the world map following the defeat of Germany in the First World War. When Germany renounced all its African territories including German Kamerun, portions of that territory were relinquished to neighbouring Chad, the Central Africa and Gabon. The remnant was part of the old German Kamerun which had been overrun by French forces from Central Africa and British forces from Nigeria. These two ex-German territories were designated as *Le Cameroun français* and British Cameroons and they became trust territories of the UN after the Second World War. It has to be

---

[1]Germany established its first official colonial presence in the Cameroon through the signing of the German-Duala Treaty, on July 12, 1884. Förster, S., Wolfgang J. Mommsen, and Ronald Edward Robinson. Bismarck, Europe, and Africa: The Berlin Africa Conference 1884-1885 and the Onset of Partition. Oxford: Oxford University Press, 1989.

explained that "German Kamerun" ceased to exist upon the end of the First World War at the Treaty of Versailles in 1919, giving rise to the mandated territories of French Cameroon and British Cameroons.

As aforementioned, these two mandated territories of the League of Nations became trust territories of the UN upon the defeat of Germany in the Second World War, with separate and distinct identities. The administering authorities signed trust agreements with the UN on 13th December 1946 and assumed responsibility to prepare their respective trust territories towards self-government or independence.

Following the Treaty of Versailles, the German territory of Kamerun was formally divided on 28 June 1919 between a French and a British League of Nations Mandate, the French acquiring 85 percent of the territory (425 000 km^2) while the English were contented with 15 percent (53000 km^2). [2] It is the share that the French received in the sharing which is here-referred to as French Cameroon. The sharing was endorsed during the peace conference of Versailles but French Cameroon ceased to be a French colony to become a territory under Mandate B of the League of Nations leaguered to France. The French administered the section of Cameroon they occupied as a territory under League of Nations [which became the UN after the Second World War] tutelage, and the British dealt with the section of the territory they occupied as part of Nigeria but with its own administration apart.

From 1916 until 1960, France administered the region of Cameroun under an assimilationist policy that hoped to transform the colonized people into French citizens. In May 1916, France issued a decree that divided the territory into nine administrative areas, each of which reported to the French Ministry of Colonies. The Ministry also established a Council of Notables in each administrative area to serve as the intermediary between the French government and the local population.

The Brazzaville Conference of 1944 addressed the political and legal rights of France's Sub-Saharan colonies. For French Cameroun, the Brazzaville Conference was a monumental start to an organized political identity. The Conference established the representation of colonies in the French National Assembly and any other parliamentary body that the new constitution would create. [3] The Conference also declared that the rights of colonial citizens were equal to those of the French and that while the colonies would remain united under the French flag, each would have a semi-autonomous assembly of its own. In 1945, French Cameroun elected its first set of representatives to the French National Assembly.

The British [1916-1945] divided the territory of Southern Cameroons into four administrative units each one under a Distinct Officer. The administrative units were Victoria, Kumba, Mamfe, and Bamenda. The District Officers were assisted in smaller administrative units by assistant District Officers.

Applying the principle of indirect rule, the British allowed native authorities to administer populations according to their own traditions. [Indirect Rule] consisted of leaving for locals [Native Authorities] the task of managing their people according to their customs on the condition that these customs did not clash with principles of British civilisation. Towards these indigenous entities the British were rather guides, reserving the essence of their efforts to the

---

[2]Elango, L.Z.. "The Anglo-French 'condominium' in Cameroon: The myth and the reality." *International Journal of African Historical Studies*: 658-710."
[3]"Ivory Coast - Brazzaville Conference." Ivory Coast - Brazzaville Conference. http://www.country-data.com/cgi-bin/query/r-6895.html Accessed on the 18/09/2018.

exploitation of economic and mineral resources and to ensuring that natives were under British legislation. These also collected taxes, which were then paid over to the British. The British devoted themselves to trade, and to exploiting the economic and mining resources of the territory.

British Cameroons were a federation of sovereign but interdependent ethnocracies, each under a traditional ruler called "*fon*" or chief: there were paramount chiefs in Buea and Victoria and *fons* in Bali, Bafut, Kom, Bum, Nso and Bangwa. The chiefs and *fons* were given the means to exercise their rule. Thus they had a court and a traditional treasury which was in charge of administrative and fiscal roles. They were in charge of the health and the education of the populations, of order and crime and in general to foster the development of their locality.

Southern Cameroons students, including Emmanuel Mbela Lifafa Endeley, created the Cameroons Youth League (CYL) on 27th March 1940, to oppose what they saw as the exploitation of their country.

When the League of Nations ceased to exist in 1946, most of the mandate territories were reclassified as UN trust territories, henceforth administered through the UN Trusteeship Council. The object of trusteeship was to prepare the lands for eventual independence. The UN approved the Trusteeship Agreements for British Cameroons to be governed by Britain on 6th December 1946 and the territory was divided in 1949 into two provinces – Bamenda (capital Bamenda, hence also thus named) and Southern (capital Buea). Yet the residential type of administration was continued with a single British Resident at Buea, but in 1949, Edward John Gibbons was appointed Special Resident, and on 1st October 1954.

Following the Ibadan General Conference of 1950, a new constitution for Nigeria devolved more power to the regions. In the subsequent election thirteen Southern Cameroonian representatives were elected to the Eastern Nigerian House of Assembly in Enugu. In 1953, however, the Southern Cameroons representatives, unhappy with the domineering attitude of Nigerian politicians and lack of unity among the ethnic groups in the Eastern Region, declared a "benevolent neutrality" and withdrew from the assembly. At a conference in London from 30th July to 22nd August 1953, the Southern Cameroons delegation asked for a separate region of its own. The British agreed, and Southern Cameroons became an autonomous region with its capital still at Buea.

1954 saw the emergence of a modern parliamentary democracy, consisting of a House of Chiefs appointed from among the traditional leaders, a House of Assembly elected by universal suffrage, and a government led by a leader of Government Business appointed and dismissed by the Queen of England. Elections were held and the parliament met on 1st October 1954, with E.M.L. Endeley as Premier.

Southern Cameroons political parties advocated different solutions to the problem of terminating the UN Trusteeship. The Cameroon National Federation (C.N.F.)[4] demanded the raising of the Southern Cameroons into a distinct and autonomous region of the Federation of Nigeria and *re*unification with French Cameroon. Not so long after however, divergences arose within the party on the question of *re*-unification. Certain party leaders, notably Narius Mbile and R. K. Dibongue were of the thinking that the party's chosen procedure on the question of *re*-unification was not spirited enough. They decided to quit the C.N.F. and created the Kamerun United National Congress (K.U.N.C). The new party had a clear programme: British and French

---

[4]The first political party, created in May 1949 by Emmanuel Endeley.

Cameroon would be united as it was the case under German control, whence the adoption of the German spelling "Kamerun" in its manifesto. The *U.P.C.* gave weight to this objective by creating cells in Southern Cameroons. In 1953, due to reconciliation between Endeley and the former members of the C.N.F., a new party, the Kamerun National Congress (K.N.C.) arose. This party won the elections of 1953 making Endeley the *leader of Government Business*.

However there were four different tendencies within the party, namely,
- Autonomists who sought autonomy within the Federation of Nigeria. Its leader was Endeley
- Secessionists who sought breaking away from Nigeria
- The third tendency was that of the *re*-unificationists who sought the *re*-unification of the two Cameroons; One Kamerun, a *U.P.C.* faction under the leadership of Ndeh Ntumazah also favoured unification of the British and French territories
- The last tendency was that of supporters of Ngu Foncha who claimed to be moderates rejecting at the same time *re*-unification and integration into Nigeria. It is this last wing which would create the Kamerun National Democratic Party (K.N.D.P.)

Despite the divergences between the political leaders of Southern Cameroons, their requests were taken seriously by the British. The British dealt with them gradually, through constitutional modifications, conferences which brought together the main protagonists, namely the British, British Cameroons and representatives of the UN Organisation.[5]

With the aim of definitively resolving the question of terminating the UN Trusteeship, the British and the UN Organisation decided to consult Cameroonians through a referendum. The question asked was to know if, yes or no, these populations wished to become Nigerians or *remain* Cameroonians in *their own* country. The third option, independence, was opposed by the UK representative to the UN Trusteeship Council, Sir Andrew Cohen, and as a result was not put. The consultations took place on the 11th February 1961 and the option for unification of the two Cameroons won in the Southern British Cameroons while the Northern British Cameroons voted for its integration in the Nigerian Federation.

The UN General Assembly as the ultimate organ of the UN, by Resolution 1608(xv) of 21st April 1961, reviewed the results of the plebiscite held in British Cameroons on 11th/12th April 1961, and made the following decisions:
1. Effective 1st June, 1961, Northern British Cameroons was to join Northern Nigeria as a separate province;
2. Southern British Cameroons was to remain a British Trust Territory until 1st October 1961 when Trustee Britain was to graduate it to Independence, in order to enable it in that capacity, to unite with independent *La République du Cameroun* to form a Confederation of two Independent States, equal in status.

A trust territory is a non-self-governing territory placed under an administrative authority by the Trusteeship Council of the United Nations. Trust territory guidelines required that the lands be prepared for independence and majority rule. At the material time British Southern Cameroons was a self-governing territory founded on the Westminster parliamentary democracy. It had been declared ripe for independence by the United Kingdom Representative to the UN and by Commissioner J. O. Field in his speech in 1958 during the Centenary celebration of the

---

[5] There was the Mamfe conference (1950), and the Conference of Lancaster House (1959).

founding of the seaport town of Victoria and had adopted its own constitution in October 1960, to usher it to independence.

For Resolution 1608 (xv) to pass the test of democracy, 64 Nations voted FOR, 23 AGAINST and 10 ABSTAINED. *La République du Cameroun*, supervised by *La République de France*, and French-speaking Africa, excepting the Republic of Mali, voted against. It was therein specified that before 1st October 1961, there was to be a tripartite Conference of the Administering Authority, the Government of the Southern Cameroons and the Government of *La République du Cameroun*, to draw up an Agreement to be signed by all three parties, embodying the terms and understandings of the joining two Cameroon parties, consistent of course with UN General Assembly Resolution 1541(xv) of 15th December, 1960 defining what is meant by *"Independence by Joining."*

Without doubt since at the time British Southern Cameroons was not a distinct UN Member state, it was the United Kingdom as the Administering Authority that was to report the outcome of the negotiations to the UN General Assembly. Indeed, it was the United Kingdom that had the political and constitutional duty of submitting the Agreement, in other words, the treaty to the UN General Secretariat in fulfillment of Article 102 of the UN Charter.

Apparently, Britain as Trustee over the Southern Cameroons, failed to initiate the move for this Conference to take place, and so the conference never held. The United Kingdom never gave a report to the UN on the implementation of Resolution 1608 (XV).

There were meetings between East Cameroonians and West Cameroonians [formerly British Southern Cameroons] to attain the ideal formula of the new being together. They met in Bamenda in June 1961, then at Foumban in July 1961 and finally in Yaounde in August, 1961. It was at Foumban [in *La République du Cameroun*] that the politicians of *La République du Cameroun* and British Southern Cameroons met to consider the last event towards unification and a constitution for the Federal Republic of Cameroon was *agreed* upon. The meeting was an informal meeting – neither Great Britain nor the UN were in attendance.

To terminate the Trusteeship Agreement, it was necessary that the Independence of the Southern Cameroons be voted by the UN. Speaking before the vote was taken in the 4th Committee of the UN General Assembly, Monsieur Traore (UN Permanent Representative of Mali) said, "If the Committee voted against the date of 1st October 1961, the Assembly would be placed in an extremely difficult position, as it would have before it a proposal requesting independence for the Southern Cameroons but not specifying any date."

Opposed to this was Monsieur Okala (Foreign Minister of *La République du Cameroun*) "Strongly protested against a vote" which he regarded as "anti-constitutional." Failing to obtain wide support, he then declared "The delegation of *Cameroun* would not participate in the vote and would withdraw – "(UN General Assembly, XV Session, Office Records, Wednesday, 19th April 1961, New York, p. 381).

The date 1st October, 1961 as Independent Day of the Southern Cameroons was put to vote. It was overwhelmingly approved by 50 "YES," 2 "NO" and 12 Abstention by the powerful 4th Committee of the UN General Assembly. 1st October was voted as Southern Cameroons Independence Day. A Trust Territory acceded to independence upon termination of trusteeship.

On September 1st 1961 the assembly of *La République du Cameroun* passed a law [law N° 24/61], unilaterally amending its constitution [to provide for annexation of Southern

Cameroons].[6] In that law and in policy statements afterwards, *La République du Cameroun* stated that the trust territory of British Southern Cameroons *is part of her territory to be returned to her* by the UN and Great Britain![7]

Ahmadou Ahidjo denied any conspiracy to absorb West Cameroon, and said there was a single Cameroon, its citizens having the same rights and duties. Then he added, significantly,

"After the people of West Cameroon massively voted in favour of re-unification and not for federation, after re-unification itself we freely estimated that it was necessary to create a federation between the two states, and to create federal institutions. But that does not permit us to say that there are two Cameroonian nations."

In the same month French-led forces of *La République du Cameroun* marched into British Southern Cameroons, *physically occupied* the territory and began enforcing a state of emergency declared on the territory.

However, these apparently were not of what the UN resolution 1608(xv) was about. The UN Resolution 1608 (XV) of April 21st, 1961 was adopted by the UN General Assembly as a follow up of the successful conduct of the UN sponsored plebiscite in the British Southern Cameroons. It was in recognition of and defense of the distinctive identity of this UN Trust territory under international law. It was a legal instrument by the World Body meant to complete the exercise of bringing together two distinct UN trust territories into a federal arrangement of equal states. The UN General Assembly Resolution above everything else testifies to the irrefutable fact that the plebiscite was inconclusive. It offered the British Southern Cameroons only an opportunity to indicate her choice between Nigeria and *La République du Cameroun*. The plebiscite was only a promise to be translated into a concrete and thorough mutual agreement based on fair negotiations.

The premature departure of the British defence forces from the Southern Cameroons on 30th September 1961, created a security void in the Southern Cameroons and it was Monsieur Ahmadou Ahidjo of *La République du Cameroun* who took the salute at Tiko airport as Commander-in-Chief of a country that had never legally joined his country *La République du Cameroun*. Senior citizens and activists for clarity on the question of the unification of the Southern Cameroons and *La République du Cameroun* affirm that *La République du Cameroun* has been in colonial occupation of the Southern Cameroons following the security void created by the departure of the British Army on 30th September 1961. This would be false if *La République du Cameroun* can show any proof of a signed agreement with the Southern Cameroons Government, promulgated into Law by the Commissioner for Cameroons who acted for the British colonial administration until 1st October 1961. In the absence of such an agreement, the so-called joining is in violation of both the UN Charter Article 102 as well as UN General Assembly Resolution 1608(xv) of 21st April. 1961.

When the *U.P.C.* began to seek independence for the UN-trusted territory of Cameroon, its chosen name for the country when it would become independent was *Kamerun* ["Cameroon" spelt in German] and taught its militants that Cameroon was *not* a French colony. Its request to the international community was that the Cameroons [the British administered component and the French-administered component] were to be *united*, a governing council and an assembly with law-making powers constituted, and a timeline of events towards independence given.

---

[6]Southern Cameroons was still under British trusteeship.
[7]Law N° 24/61, promulgated by her president on September 1 1961.

Apparently this was a normal request; the two entities used to be one and for viability, the bigger the country at independence, the better. Actually, the *U.P.C.* had been incensed by French non-wish to grant independence to French colonies. The *U.P.C*'s request for *re*-unification was its reminder to the international community that Cameroon was *not* a French colony. Cameroon was a UN-trusted territory administered under French and British tutelage. The political development of the territory was the concern of the UN: it was incumbent on the UN and not on the French or on the British to grant independence to Cameroon. On this reminder, the French tried to change the status of the territory under Trusteeship but stumbled against *U.P.C.* mass education: whence the decision and scheme to implement their own agenda. To maintain total control over the natural resources and the political development of the country, the French *decided* on, planned, and carried out a *pogrom*; all Cameroonians to the last militant of the U.P.C. who had come to know and believed that Cameroon was not a French colony and were not willing to change their beliefs were hunted down and were to be killed, beginning from 1955. When they thought that they had sufficiently weakened the movement for an independent Cameroon which would not be under French control, killing the *mpodol*, they granted internal autonomy to French Cameroon.

The French would not grant freedom and independence to the territories which constituted their colonies. When their position on the issue became untenable, they were *obligated* to negotiate autonomy and formal independence. For the specific case of Cameroon, they *schemed* political independence for *La République du Cameroun* which implied continued though submerged French control of public life and unfettered access to the natural resources of Cameroon. This would later be christened neo-colonialism.

Southern Cameroons on the other hand, continued as a trust territory under British Administration.

There has been a *unification* according to *the wish of majority* of the people of Cameroon – the wish of the people of *La République du Cameroun* was taken for granted, while that of Southern British Cameroons was read in the *direct votes* of inhabitants of the then British southern Cameroons. That there were no plebiscite elections in the French-administered territory can be interpreted as follows: it might have been supposed that *elected representatives*, since it was an independent republic already, spoke for her. This could lead some to think that it was *La République du Cameroon* which took British Southern Cameroons into the republic. Wrong: it is in record that *La République du Cameroun*, dictated to by the French, actually voted *against* unification in a UN General Assembly vote on the question.[1]

On occasion, on the issue of the UN vote, the position of *La République du Cameroun* was that Cameroon was already an independent country. There was no question of independence for British Cameroons. Rather, she was requesting that the UN and Britain restitute territory which she *claimed* has always been part of *La République du Cameroun*. The result of that vote [lost by *La République du Cameroun*] led to the UN decision of 1st October, 1961 as the future date for the independence of former British Southern Cameroons. As the British Under-Secretary of State for the Colonies, Mr. Hugh Fraser, explained in the House of Commons on 1st August, 1961, "it is a question both of granting independence and of creating a new unit from the Cameroon Republic[2] and the Southern Cameroons"[3]

It is clear beyond conjecture that *La République du Cameroun* had contracted to receive *West Cameroons* as an *equal sovereign state* and at one and the same time to form with it a federation of *two equal sovereign* states.[4] *La République du Cameroun* had agreed that the sovereign powers shall be transferred to an organisation representing the future federation. Since the state of West Cameroon will be a *sovereign*, independent state equal in all respects to the *République*, it is necessary that the organisation representing the future federation shall be composed of equal elements representing the *La République du Cameroun* and the state of West Cameroon. It is not compatible with the dignity of West Cameroon that the organisation should be the President of *La République du Cameroun* acting in association with the Head of State of West Cameroon.[5]

In order that the people of West Cameroon may achieve independence by joining *La République du Cameroun* it is necessary that the federation should come into existence at midnight of 1st October. At one and the same moment there will be born the independent state of the West Cameroon and the federation of the United Kamerun Republic. The federation would be a free association of independent and equal sovereign states.

In October 1966, an incident occurred, illustrative of Augustine Ngom Jua's[6] determination to defend the territorial integrity of West Cameroon. On 1st October 1966, Emmanuel Epie, editor of the *Cameroon Mirror,* published a lead story captioned 'Federal regions may be re-carved'. The paper stated that Ahmadou Ahidjo planned to re-carve administrative regions in

---

[1] UN Organisation Resolution 1608(XV), 21st April, 1961. 64 nations voted for the independence of Southern Cameroons.
[2] *La République du Cameroun.*
[3] CO554/2260 XE 4120.
[4] PRO CO554/2188X3406 June 1961.
[5] Ibid., See Jacques Benjamin, p. 60.
[6] The sitting Prime Minister, leader of the majority party in the West Cameroon parliament at the time.

such a way that the result would be the extinction of West Cameroon as a distinct and separate cultural, political, and legal unit.

According to the report West Cameroon would be cut up into several parts, each of which would then be fused into the region in *La République du Cameroun* closest to it. In the planned reconfiguration part of Victoria Division would be incorporated into *Département du Wouri* of *Région du Littoral*, and Kumba Division would be merged with *Département du Moungo*. As part of *Région de l'Ouest*, Mamfe Division would be swallowed up by *Département de la Menoua*, and Bamenda and Wum Divisions would be fused with *Département de la* Mifi. As part of *Région du Nord*, Nkambe Division would be integrated into *Département du Banyo*.

Jua's reaction to this alarming news was swift and robust. In a statement issued to the press he declared:

> *"It must be emphasised that the Federal Republic of Cameroon is a federation of two states with different backgrounds, cultures and traditions; the present arrangement was in fact envisaged as the most ideal solution to reunification ... Any exercise, therefore, that is designed to alter this arrangement ... will clearly alter the basis on which the entire federation rests and will throw our present system of government into complete disarray ... It is equally clear that since ours is a democratic republic a matter of far-reaching significance and consequences cannot be conceived and executed in secret without the full knowledge and concurrence of the people of West Cameroon through their accredited representatives, to wit, the West Cameroon Government."*

Whatever the case, Jua had made his point. There could be no question of a unilateral alteration of the well-known frontier between the two component states of the informal federation without the concurrence of the people of West Cameroon acting through their democratically elected Government. It was clearly implied in Jua's press statement that such concurrence would not be forthcoming as that would alter the very basis of the federal association, though informal, and put the federation itself asunder.

In January 1968, Ahmadou Ahidjo, in complete disregard of the constitutional conventions of West Cameroon, appointed Solomon Tandeng Muna to replace Jua as Prime Minister in Buea, much to the universal consternation and chagrin in West Cameroon. The people of West Cameroon were devastated. For most of them Muna's appointment was nothing short of a *coup d'état*.

Muna's government in Buea was characterised by his espousal of 'centralist federalism', indistinguishable from Ahmadou Ahidjo's 'unitary federalism' [curious term]. It was heavily tilted [eastwards], towards *La République du Cameroun*, and was perceived by political watchers as a mere agency of Ahmadou Ahidjo's dictatorship.

Then in October 1968, he signed a decree placing West Cameroon Police Force under his direct authority, in flagrant violation of the constitution of the federated state. In a continuing effort to eliminate all reality of the autonomy of West Cameroon, in 1970 Ahmadou Ahidjo 'federalised' West Cameroon Police Force, that is to say, he fused it into the Camerounese police force known as 'Sureté Naiionale'.

Ahmadou Ahidjo moved in 1969 to further strengthen 'territorial administration', that is, restrict still further whatever autonomy West Cameroon still had left. He increased the power exercisable by the '*préfets*' and the '*inspecteurs*'. The extensive powers they had included the power: to order the torture of individuals as a means of forcing compliance with their every command; to order the indefinite detention of persons, such order not subject to enquiry by any court of law; to order the confiscation of people's property, such order not also subject to question by any court of law; and to order the suspension of freedom of the press, of expression, of information, of movement (of persons and goods), and of assembly and association, without due process of law. The '*préfets*' and '*gouverneurs*' continue to enjoy these arbitrary powers to this day, unchecked by law.

There was one nagging problem of capital importance to the autonomy of West Cameroon. It concerned the revenue of the state. Jua boldly made efforts to resolve this problem. A gaping lacuna in Ahmadou Ahidjo's federal constitution was that the principle of revenue allocation was not included in its provisions. In other words, no provision was made for revenue sharing between federal and state governments. This was deliberate. The biggest sources of West Cameroon's revenue were customs and excise duty and export of cash crops.

By order of Ahmadou Ahidjo all the revenue from these critical sources went entirely and directly into the coffers of the federal government in Yaounde. For example, West Cameroon taxes amounted to FCFA 418 million and licenses 125 million in the 1966-67 fiscal year, taxes 647 million and licenses 130 million in the 1968-69 fiscal year. This money went to Yaounde. West Cameroon was therefore deprived of its main sources of revenue. As a result Buea depended on Yaounde to subsidise its budget. Jua requested the federal government for there to be negotiated a permanent system of revenue allocation, a fixed and secure source of revenue. Ahmadou Ahidjo refused and he also refused to allow the government of West Cameroon any significant financial autonomy.

Jua then tried to set up a mechanism for auto-financing. He described as "a hazardous adventure" the system by which Ahmadou Ahidjo granted an annual subsidy to cover the budgeted expenditures of West Cameroon to make up the deficit over income, since West Cameroon government could not tell in advance the amount which it would please Ahmadou Ahidjo to make available to it. This was a system deliberately created by Ahmadou Ahidjo. Its objective was to cast West Cameroon in the mould of a beggar and to leave its government at the mercy of *La République du Cameroun*. "These *ad hoc* subsidies are thoroughly unsatisfactory," lamented in 1966 P.M. Kemcha, who was then both Finance Minister and Deputy Prime Minister of West Cameroon.

Jua wondered aloud: "How can a State develop by itself according to its priorities if it cannot know how much it has at its disposal?" He then proposed to Ahmadou Ahidjo that there be set up a Joint Allocation Committee to decide in a permanent manner the sharing out of public revenue between the component governments of the Federation. "Otherwise," he added, "the [West Cameroon] Government would not be able to hold out for long as a real government, taking decisions itself in areas over which it enjoys sovereignty."

This was precisely the level to which Ahmadou Ahidjo wanted to reduce West Cameroon. So he rejected Jua's proposal. He was bent on inducing a dependency syndrome in West Cameroon, on weakening the government of West Cameroon and on promoting the fiction that West Cameroon could not survive without *La République du Cameroun*. Ahmadou Ahidjo would in 1972 turn round and advance West Cameroon's alleged poverty as one of the reasons for his scrapping of the Federation and his formal annexation of West Cameroon.

By decree on 20th October 1968, Ahmadou Ahidjo reorganised the federal territory into six administrative regions including West Cameroon, and appointed a Federal Inspector for each region, who was to report to the Federal President. That provoked discontent among Anglophones because West Cameroon could not at the same time be a federated state according to the constitution and an administrative region by decree. The Federal Inspector had more power than the elected Prime Minister of West Cameroon and showed it on a daily basis by humiliating members of the federated government and parliament [of West Cameroon]. Thus, by other means than diplomacy, *La République du Cameroun* set out to acquire former British Southern Cameroons.

As a matter of fact, considering violation by *La République du Cameroun* of UN Resolution 1608 of the 21st April, 1961, the Southern Cameroons could still be considered to date as a UN Trust territory. Such a Trust was not anymore under the United Kingdom according to the 13th December, 1946 agreement but under *La République du Cameroun* through its police, gendarmerie, army, administration, tax services and customs, etc.[7]

The colonial powers grabbed and patched together territories belonging to the peoples of Africa, often territories containing groups who had been rivals and even bitter enemies for centuries. They called these territories countries. In the colonial administrative systems, governance followed a "from the top down" approach which was largely arbitrary. The immediate purpose of the colonial government was to control the population and ensure the continuous exploitation of natural resources for the benefit of the colonising powers. This purpose was met with authoritarian rule and bolstered by a strong police and soldiers with guns.

Power rested with the colonial authorities who maintained their authoritarian status with force; consequently, *political legitimacy* was attached to the unequivocal control of force. Colonialism implanted the notion that authoritarianism is an appropriate mode of political rule and that force is an acceptable instrument of that rule. These features of the colonial system were the most characteristic of French colonies. It is to these legacies and the circumstances in which French Cameroon attained formal independence that explanation of the approach of the leadership of the emergent *La République du Cameroun* may be traced.

As a matter of fact, *La République du Cameroun* which emerged from the *territoire sous tutelle* was a neo-colonial state. Ahmadou Ahidjo did not have any claim to a national mandate at the time of his accession to power (when he replaced Andre-Marie Mbida in February 1958) for the fact that the legislative Assembly was *the* assembly elected under conditions of boycott and violence in December 1956. Actually there was the question of legislative elections to be conducted in the territory in 1958, after the slaying of Ruben Um Nyobe. The French through their diplomacy at the UN, thwarted the event and went on with their plans to award *independence*, determined that it would be so even if it meant killing everybody. Elections – a scheme of rigging to ensure that power remained in the control and exercise of individuals who must be submissive and loyal to the Republic of France – were held only after independence. As the date for the proclamation of independence drew close, for most of Cameroon, the streets were strewn with corpses.

The atrocities of French colonial wars are rightly, the legacies of the French Right. Apparently, with the coming to power of the Socialist Party of France, in 1981 the Ahmadou Ahidjo regime French political advisers would quickly be out of work. Left to himself after 24 years in power, Ahmadou Ahidjo's *ineptitude* will not be long to come to the fore.

The regime of Ahmadou Ahidjo (1960-1982) – a continuation of the colonial regime – for want of legitimacy, was ultra-repressive. It readily resorted to the arbitrary and to brutality even in

---

[7] Hence the present struggle of the peoples of the Southern Cameroons for independence no more by joining with *La République du Cameroun* to form a Federal State which the regime in Yaoundé does not want, but towards the creation of a state known as Ambazonia.

parts of Cameroon which were remote from the activities of the banned *U.P.C.* and long after all of its following had been coerced [arrested and tortured] to switch loyalty in favour of the regime, choose exile and live permanently in fear of assassination, or killed.

Talking about the Ahmadou Ahidjo regime, the things we would say, perhaps with some exaggeration beyond the ideal-type, could be said in the inverse with the same passion, to characterise in pure essence, the regime of a widely revered contemporary of his, Julius Nyerere of Tanzania. The Ahmadou Ahidjo regime is *perhaps* an empirical instance where it could be said that the leader drew from the dark side[8]...! The political order in Cameroon under Ahmadou Ahidjo was sustained by a strong military presence, an all-pervading secret service, the brutal repression of any form of political dissent and the use of torture in near concentration camp conditions, reformation camps for opponents to the regime and a rigid censorship of all forms of expression.[9] A dictatorship arose out of what the French put in place as the leadership for *La République du Cameroun* which did everything to hide the circumstances in which it got to power and the interest it served, exerting itself to erase all thoughts and memories of the *U.P.C.* The objective of the French was to physically eliminate the *U.P.C.*, but especially, to eradicate emancipatory ideas (including the thought at all of being opponents of the regime) it had put in the minds of the people. As military resistance diminished, the psychological action was extended to the entirety of the population: radio and news paper propaganda [equating the *U.P.C.* with the tsetse fly, film screenings, village fairs and dances], brain washing, wordy talks to lead the population away, to forget that she had been robbed of independence some had fought for with plenty of ardour.

Emmanuel Endeley on the eve of the February 1961 plebiscite had warned Southern Cameroonians that, "If you vote for Cameroun Republic, you will invite a new system under which everyone lives in fear of the police and army. You will not be free to move about; you cannot lecture freely or discuss your political views in public; ... and you can be arrested and flogged by the police and even imprisoned without a fair trial."

> *"Who amongst you," he asked, "would like to live in French Cameroun, a country red with the blood of thousands of innocent victims killed by terrorists and the Ahidjo regime...who amongst you will like to live in a country which lacks complete respect for human dignity and where you cannot speak out your mind freely or pursue your business in peace... Who amongst you will like your children to grow up in servitude? ... That will be our lot if we join French Cameroun."*

Journalists who dared to criticise the administration were "disappeared." Their papers were confiscated and people dared not to get early morning copies. Their homes could be searched and they themselves made to suffer physically.[10]

> *Often, on the basis of an anonymous denunciation, the local "Gestapo" (policemen of the SEDOC)[11] came at three o'clock in the morning to seize someone brutally in the midst of his dazed family who were then ordered to keep quiet... Cruel reprisals were perpetrated against poor villagers who had handed over their foodstuffs, fearing the pillage if not incarceration of the village if they refused. The army arrived the following day: "You have helped the rebels, you'll see what that's going to cost," and then was the*

---

[8]Hollywood neologism in the movie titled "Star wars."

[9] Richard Joseph, (1977). *Radical nationalism in Cameroon*, Oxford: Clarendon Press, pp. 49- 50.

[10] Ibid., Eden Xtra, p. 50 Paul Kode, "The Cameroon press in retrospect."

[11] *Service des Études et de Documentation.*

plundering, the daughters raped, the children beaten, the wives stripped naked and whipped ... (Joseph, 1978: 96).[12]

Excepting censorship relating to expression of dissent, though considerably attenuated, the methods of the Ahidjo regime are still present so many years since his resignation[13] for *personal reasons* long after the lifting of the regime of exception of the *insurrection* years: frequent, impressive and suggestive special paramilitary forces in the city centres of Yaoundé, Douala and other major cities even when there are no events of social movements which would require the response of such forces, highly "militarised" nature of day-to-day politics, the active participation of special forces [*forces de défense et de sécurité*] in the policing of the society, and the use of deadly force [live ammunitions and helicopter gunships] in very improbable spaces like university campuses, supermarkets and moving urban crowds on bridges and against isolated individuals who prefer to stay indoors or go to their farms to avoid streets protests where they could get injured.[14]

Whence the suggestion of *domestic colonialism* [Cameroonians as subjects to the personnel in power as administered populations] – military occupation – in the approach to issues of administration and governance in the so-called united republic of Cameroon of today. Members of government and those who are under them through to the lowest state functionary pay allegiance to Paul Biya, *le Chef de l'État*, and carry out their duties *selon la volonté du Président de La République*. This reality is rather stark in the territories of former British Southern Cameroons: deliberately, more than 90 percent of civil administrators appointed to serve in the English-speaking parts of Cameroon originate from the French-speaking part of the county. The Anglophone Cameroonian, when he considers his heritage in relation to civil administration and political practice, finds himself in some land of *surprises* in his *own* country.

In June 1990 the Anglophone architect of the federal state John Ngu Foncha resigned as First Vice President of the *RDPC*.[15] He explained that: The Anglophone Cameroonians whom he brought into the union have been ridiculed and referred to as "*les Biafrais*," "*les ennemis dans la maison*," "*les traitres*" etc., and the constitutional provisions which protected this Anglophone minority have been suppressed, *their voice drowned* while the rule of the gun replaced the dialogue which the Anglophones cherish very much.[16] As it is, former British Southern Cameroons has *disappeared*.

The leadership in *La République du Cameroun* arose from French choice as we said and to a large extent very little democratic practices have ever been tried in the system since decolonisation. Specifically, *La République du Cameroun* has never had a *genuinely* democratically voted in President of the Republic, and representatives in the national assembly since its decolonisation. Thomas Deltombe, Manuel Domergue and Jacob Tatsitsa quote in *Kamerun!* "the former colonial administrator Guy Georgy, who recalled with pride how he had plucked Ahidjo, then working for the postal service, from obscurity at the age of 23, stuffing ballot boxes to get him into the Territorial Assembly in 1947."[17]

---

[12]Submission credited to M. Charles Van de Lanoitte in Joseph, Richard (Ed.) (1978). *Gaullist Africa: Cameroon under Ahmadou Ahidjo*. Enugu: Fourth Dimension Publishers. P. 96.

[13]Paul Biya, who was Ahmadou Ahidjo's Prime Minister, became President of the Republic [without elections] in November, 1982.

[14]2008 food riots in Douala.

[15]RDPC for *Rassemblement Démocratique du Peuple Camerounais* – the name for the *Union Nationale Cameounaise* (*UNC*) party after the resignation and disgrace of Ahmadou Ahidjo.

[16]John Ngu Foncha's letter of resignation from the RDPC is reproduced in Mukong (ed.), p.155.

[17]Source: Augusta_Conchiglia_Ghosts of Kamerun_NHR 77_September-October 2012.Pdf.

The constitution of *La République du Cameroun* "submitted to a referendum in February, 1960 passed thanks to patent fraud: the 'No' option received 95 per cent of the vote in Douala and 90 in Yaoundé, but there was an 80 per cent 'Yes' from the Bamileké region, whose villages were being strafed by French aircraft at the time."[18] Twice, in 1965 and in 1970, Ahmadou Ahidjo was elected with 100 percent of the vote, and was the only candidate for presidential elections in 1975 and 1980.

The constitution has repeatedly been modified apparently after votes in the parliament but really by fiat notably [in the period of negotiations towards the suppression of the federal system], regarding the procedure to be followed in the choosing of the Prime Minister. It was not necessary for the President to order the manipulation of the voting in any election. Administrative authorities, party officials, and the police made it their business to understand from his declarations the results needed and then achieve them by whatever means necessary.

When for instance Ahmadou Ahidjo taking everyone by surprise, announced on May 6th 1972 that within three weeks a *referendum* would be held on the question of abolishing a federal State, it, in effect, meant as it happened that, within three weeks a Unitary State would be established with an overwhelming "Yes" vote! The *referendum* was merely symbolic: the options were a *"Oui"* and a "Yes!"[19]

This definitely violated an important clause of the 1961 constitution of living together, namely, clause 1 of article 47 of the Foumban Accords which read: 'any proposal for the revision of the present constitution, which impairs the unity and integrity of the *Federation* shall be inadmissible." Even if the constitution were to be amended it would not be done by referendum, because clause 3 of article 47 stipulated 'that proposals for revision shall be adopted by simple majority vote of the members of the Federal Assembly, provided that such majority includes a majority of the representatives ... of *each* of the *Federated States.*[20]

A second violation would happen in 1984 when the name of the state was changed from *La République Unie du Cameroun"* to *"La République du Cameroun."*

When the *Etat sous tutelle française* became independent, she was called *"La République du Cameroun."* It is with *"La République du Cameroun"* that the Southern British Cameroons negotiated the terms of reunification. The Southern British Cameroons became the state of West Cameroon in the Federal Republic which arose from the negotiations. The change of name of the state in 1984 – the abandoning of *"La République Unie du Cameroun,"* to *"La République du Cameroun"* – was perceived in many circles as a simple phagocytising of the old West Cameroon by the old East Cameroon [*La République du Cameroun*], within the Federal Republic.[21]

Politically, Anglophone Cameroon had not had the tumultuous independence struggle of *le territoire sous tutelle*. It can be argued that it had had some sure experience of democratic practices in the choosing of its leaders and in processes of law-making. The British mandate/trust territory, which came to be called the Southern British Cameroons, was initially attached to the

---

[18]Ibid.

[19]"Oui" is French for "Yes." So the possible votes were "Yes" in French, and "Yes" in English.

[20]Mukong, A. W. (ed.) (1990). The case for Southern Cameroons, Yaounde, *Cameroon Federalist Committee* p. 18.

[21]Submission credited to David Abouèm à Tchoyi: published on the WWW on 09/01/2017.

Eastern Provinces of Nigeria up till 1954; in 1958, it achieved a regional status and a limited degree of self-government,[22] within the Federation of Nigeria.

Emmanuel Endeley progressively moved from a pre-*re*-unification stand towards a more positive view on integration, which meant that the inhabitants could rule themselves, maintain their ties to the British inheritance, and avoid the violence and chaos of civil war in francophone Cameroon. In a policy statement in 1958 he said:

> *Most of us have at one time or the other, advocated the ultimate unification of the French and the British Cameroons as it was before the 1914-1918 war. While we still hold this view, new events and circumstances have overtaken us, and have removed the question of unification out of the realm of urgency and priority in which we had earlier placed it. With the northern Cameroons absorbed into northern Nigeria, and French Cameroons assimilated into the French Union, it now seems unlikely that Cameroon would ever return to the status it was before 1914. The advocates of immediate unification appear to overlook these facts and still have to show to the world how they propose, in the interest of peace and prosperity of all the sections concerned, to achieve their aim. We of the government however, having the political, economic and social well being of the Southern Cameroons uppermost in our minds, are convinced that far from being a priority issue, unification should only be achieved by evolutionary means, that is, when an independent French Cameroons outside the French Union, and an independent Nigerian Federation of which the Southern Cameroons will form a part, would be in an unfettered position to explore the possibilities of Union as part of the movement towards the creation of a united states of West Africa. We are not prepared to forgo the safeguards and benefits which we now enjoy as a member of the Federation, in preference to an unstable and unpredictable French Union.*[23]

When he lost crucial electoral battles of 1959-1961, John Ngu Foncha replaced him as Prime Minister.

In British administered Cameroon, the colonial administration seemed distant, and authority and power were exercised through local chiefs: power and authority are perceived in British administered Cameroon as the preserve of the people. The House of Chiefs was a key component in the administration of Anglophone Cameroon.

A positive aspect of British approach in their enterprise of Empire building, was the emphasis on the force of augment and the use of the ballot box and not the gun. In the process of decolonisation they remote-censored the desires of the nationalists which were defused constitutionally.

The cultures of administration inherited from English colonial experience thrives on the principle of the responsabilisation of different levels of social organisation. Considered side by side with what had been the case for *le territoire sous tutelle*, where the tendency was towards hypercentalisation, the challenge after decolonisation, of attaining a blend in any future was foreseeable.

---

[22]A ledge of what theorists christened "indirect rule" during the colonial era – in the administration of peoples the British ruled through the existing indigenous institutions at various levels of the society which reported to administrative officers.

[23]Policy statement on the UNIFICATION ISSUE by Premier of Southern Cameroons, Dr. E.M.L. Endeley at the state banquet held in the Mountain Hotel Buea on Thursday, May 29, 1958.
Source: Summit Magazine N° 22 October- December 2013, p. 22.

So, the Anglophone problem is a sort of development. The point of departure would be an issue or issues around which people are mobilised. If the point is missed, some would think that it would suffice to [dispatch ministers for special duties to do business with named persons (money bags which move hands, mysterious handshakes said to affect the mental abilities of people one meets), arrest people here and there], isolate individuals who have been mobilised, to deal with the Anglophone problem. This would be a mistaken view – a reduction of a *social movement* to criminal violence. Criminal violence can be traced to individual perpetrators. Social movements, which may lead to violence, are driven by issues around which constituencies have been mobilised. To diffuse the crisis that the Anglophone problem now amounts to, the path must be backwards first, to have a thorough grasp of the issue or issues around which individuals have been mobilised and then a *tracking* of the developments which led to the problem. Blind? No. Blinded? Not so sure. If for the personnel in authority, everything else would be subordinate to the sole wish to be in power and continue to be in power whatever else may happen, this can be likened to some sort of blindness.

There definitely is an issue or are issues. But what is or are the issues? The issue or issues seen clearly, the other question, and no less an important question would be whether the personnel in authority in Cameroon [Francophone component and Anglophone *sympathisers* among them] of today has the resources in terms of quality of mind, ethical maturity and especially, in terms of legitimacy it takes. To answer this other question also requires a backward movement, to have a true gasp of what is the fact of that political leadership in Cameroon. We have to examine the circumstances in which it arose, and whether beyond 1960 there has been some evolution in the terms we mentioned in the personnel to which the management of the trusted territory which became *La République du Cameroon* was leaguered – the banning of the *U.P.C.* in 1955; the legislative elections of 1956; independence for *La République du Cameroun;* mass killings in the Sanaga Maritime Region; decolonisation and independence for the *State* of *West Cameroon*; 1961 Unification of the State of West Cameroon and of *La République du Cameroun*; mass killings in Bamiléké country; 1972 Unification of the State of West Cameroon and of *La République du Cameroun*; 1985 change of the name of the single party, Cameroon National Union to Cameroon People's Democratic Movement; 1990 authorisation of the formation of other political parties; and *la tripartite.*

Issues, and more issues, and difficult issues.

The ban on syndicate leaders, the suspension of Internet connectivity for sections of the country, the creation of negotiating commissions comprising of civil servants [administrators] to consider issues which cannot be dissociated from the political, *utterances* here and there, calling people who have been mobilised names, do not seem to us to be pertinent options.

Two narratives on the status of the Southern Cameroons: The first is, for *La République du Cameroun*, on 1st October, 1961, the international community gave back to *La République du Cameroun*, a territory which belonged to her, but which was still under British tutelage after 1st January 1960 when she gained her independence. The purports to this narrative are as follows: in the UN special session on Trust Territories of 1959, the UN ordered the United Kingdom to enact an independent constitution for the Cameroons [its territories under the United Kingdom tutelage]. The United Kingdom enacted the Southern Cameroons constitution which took effect on the 1st October 1960 as the constitution of Nigeria at independence. She withdrew from Nigeria but held on to the Southern Cameroons. She would later manipulate the UN to impose a plebiscite for the peoples of the Southern Cameroons to choose either to be absorbed in Nigeria, or join *La République du Cameroun* in a confederation of two sovereign nations. The peoples of the Southern Cameroons voted for a confederation. The UN fixed the 30th October 1961 for the United Kingdom to quit the territory. But, unknown to anyone, the United Kingdom had vowed against independence fearing that an independent Southern Cameroons would nationalise the Cameroon Development Corporation (CDC)[1] in which she had invested £2,000,000. In exchange for the right to continue to exploit the CDC, the United Kingdom sold the territory of the Southern Cameroons to France, to be annexed to the *République du Cameroun*. So, while the peoples of the Southern Cameroons looked forward to celebrating independence on 1st October, 1961, French Cameroon troops moved into the territory on the 27th September, 1961 and the United Kingdom troops left, leaving the territory under French Cameroon troops to the present date.

The second narrative is that; West Cameroon voted for *independence* first and foremost and, as an eventuality, for political association in a *federal* union. There was no such thing as voting in favour of '*re-unification*'. That term does not appear in any UN records bearing on the plebiscite: there was no such option in the plebiscite as 're-unification'.[24] The framers of the plebiscite questions used the term 'to join'. By common agreement between West Cameroon and *La République du Cameroun*, well before the plebiscite, that expression was understood to mean 'to federate'. Both parties committed themselves to a federal form of political association. Statements by government ministers in the *Cameroon Times* newspaper and the contents of the *UN-SANCTIONED OFFICIAL CAMPAIGN PAMPHLET*, *The Two Alternatives*, informed the electorate that 'to join' meant 'to federate' and the electorate went to the polls with that in mind. The people of West Cameroon therefore voted in favour of *independence and federal political association*. On 1st October, 1961, the UN tutelage in the Trust territory ended and the territory joined *La République du Cameroun* as a sovereign entity with distinct boarders, to form the Federal Republic of Cameroon. The so-called Anglophone question is about the basis of the presence of *La République du Cameroun*'s presence on the territory of the former British Southern Cameroons.

The solution to the present impasse[25] is for *La République du Cameroon* to engage the people of Southern Cameroons to agree on mutually acceptable terms of association, under the auspices of some credible regional entity, perhaps with the endorsement of the UN. If the parties have been living together in harmony, there should be no great difficulty in reaching an agreement. If however they fail to reach agreement, they would revert peacefully to their respective positions.[26]

Anglophone Cameroonians could *not* have bargained to share the fortune of a people whose fortune led to the imposition on then of a leadership which had no qualms with the considerations their masters of yesterday had for them and not be able to want anything else once the deal was done including the possibility of a withdrawal in case the situation tended to or turned out to be unbearable. The leadership foisted by the French on *La République du Cameroun* (-1960), which *never gained nor even sought* legitimacy, probably believes that, like the French, it can also impose and should impose.

More than once we have had a wonderful opportunity! For the first time, we think of the 1985 *party-State* (the Cameroon National Union) Congress which was held in Bamenda. A high-

---

[24]'*Re-unification*' is not a legal term of art. The term was never used during the plebiscite campaigns. The political expression that was sometimes used during the plebiscite politicking was 'unification'.

[25]2017.

[26]Submission attributed to Mola Njoh Litumbe, an active proponent for the estuation of Statehood for former British Southern Cameroons.

profile lawyer trained in the Anglo-Saxon tradition, *fon* Gorji Dinka addressed a letter to Paul Biya[27] in which he proposed the transformation of the Congress into a forum for the reconstruction of the institutions of Cameroon. The letter was dated March 20th 1985. That letter was simply ignored. The lawyer would be arrested shortly after when he circulated a statement declaring the Paul Biya government to be *unconstitutional* calling for the independence of Southern Cameroons as the Republic of Ambazonia.[28] The name Ambazonia was used in 1984 by *fon* Gorji Dinka, when the parliament and government of La République du Cameroun changed the name of the country from the "United Republic of Cameroon" to the pre-unification name of the French Cameroun, the *"République du Cameroun."* In the view of some, particularly in the former British Cameroon, this meant a dissolution of the 1961 personal union. It was in this light that beginning in 1984, Ambazonia, was declared to represent a timely intervention of the people of the Southern Cameroons to return the statehood of the former British Southern Cameroons territory. Ambazonia saw this not as the fait accompli of a one Cameroon state, but as an opportunity to engage both states into a 'constitutional review' of their post-1984 relations. Ambazonia believed that by "operation of the law," there should be an equal participation by the two states that made up the now extinct federation, in a new vision for their countries (*République du Cameroun* and the Southern Cameroons) relation with each other. In 1992, *fon* Gorji Dinka, on behalf of the state of Republic of Ambazonia filed a lawsuit against *La République du Cameroun* and President Paul Biya on the main charge of the *République du Cameroun*'s illegal and forcible occupation since the 1984 dissolution of the United Republic of Cameroon and the declaration of the Republic of Ambazonia. This suit was registered with the Bamenda High Court in the Northwest Region of Cameroon as case number HCB28/92. Conflicting reports exist relating to the outcome of this case. However, the plaintiff, *fon* Gorji Dinka, maintains that the Bamenda High Court reached a decision according to which the court among other things held that "(b) President Paul Biya is [also] guilty of treason for furthering and completing the treason of Ahidjo by bringing about the secession of the first defendant (East Cameroon) from the United Republic of Cameroon on February 4, 1984, reinstating its name *"République du Cameroun"* which had not been used since January 10, 1961. (c) That the break-away *République du Cameroun* continues, illegally and forcibly occupy the territory of the first plaintiff, which means the first defendant is guilty of an international offence of aggression and annexation, (d). The report made the *Restoration* of the statehood of the first plaintiff the starting point of restoration of legality." Followers of the Ambazonia pressure group led by *fon* Gorji Dinka assert that this decision was published in a Cameroon newspaper, *"Le Messager"*: Vol. II No. 04 of February 10, 1993. The other opportunity was in the 1990s – from April 1991 to January 1992 – when the opposition parties in Cameroon issued calls, ultimatums, tracts, etc., asking the public to immobilise the economy by staying indoors, blocking streets, refusing to pay taxes and bills, and boycotting the markets and offices. The 'ghost town' campaigns aimed at forcing the government to hold a *conférence nationale souveraine*. With effrontery Yaoundé would respond with yet a further heightening of the militarisation of political life. To Paul Biya and his advisers, *"la conférence nationale souveraine est sans objet."* He would go on to stand for election as President of the Republic, and get himself declared winner in October 1992 in spite of difficult to hide indications of the contrary.

---

[27]From the position of Prime Minister, according to the constitution of Cameroon at the time, Paul Biya became President of the Republic in 1982 when seemingly in a condition of acute depression, Ahmadou Ahidjo resigned.

[28]See *fon* Gorji Dinka's "The new social order," dated 20 March 1985, addressed to Biya at the Bamenda *Union Nationale Camerounaise* party Congress, and his accompanying letter.

We wish to speculate on the options for the International Community on the situation in the Southern Cameroons. Perhaps the Southern Cameroons should continue to be part of the Union which arose from the plebiscite of 1961. A plebiscite indicated the choice of Southern Cameroonians at that time. The procedure towards the final arrangement is what has led to the situation of conflict of today.

The basics are that, British Southern Cameroons, in good faith entered *freely* in a unity arrangement with La République du Cameroun with the *clear understanding* that her individuality and cultural characteristics would be protected by a basic law and the International Community. 1st October, 1961 was understood, with clarification, that British Southern Cameroons would *join La République du Cameroun* and attain independence as a state [equal in status with the state of *La République du Cameroun*] in a Federal Republic.

British Southern Cameroons voted for unification with *La République du Cameroun* to become one of two states (*La République du Cameroun*, and the state of West Cameroon) with a separate legislature, judiciary, and police, of the Federal Republic of Cameroon.

The Prime Minister of British Southern Cameroons wanted British Southern Cameroons if it joined the *République du Cameroun*: "To be in effect autonomous over a very large part of the field… leaving only a few things to be dealt with by the central government or republic."[29] As suggested above, this was not the position of the *République du Cameroun*. It is in record that [Ahmadou Ahidjo], the President of La République du Cameroun pointedly affirmed that:

> "It is the view of *La République du Cameroun* that after 1st October, 1961 and pending the establishment of the federal government, those powers which will become federal would be transmitted to the President of the Republic who would exercise them in association with the Prime Minister of the Southern Cameroons."[30]

The latter position, as a matter of fact was not in accordance with the UN Resolution 2013 on Southern Cameroons. In other words it meant that:

> "If at midnight [1st October, 1961] the sovereignty of Southern Cameroons is transmitted to *La République du Cameroun* the people of the Southern Cameroons do not at that moment achieve independence. They lose their identity and become subjects of *La République du Cameroun*. It may be that within a matter of minutes, hours or days the *République* will by an act of state transform itself into a federation of two states composed of the former *République du Cameroun* and the former Southern Cameroons would then have achieved independence not by joining *La République du Cameroun* but *after* joining *La République du Cameroun*."[31]

In consultations towards effective *unification* with *La République du Cameroun*,[32] the main political leaders in British Southern Cameroons met in Bamenda in June 1961 to decide upon their own version of Federalism for a Unified Cameroon. The consensus among them included:

    i) a separate government
    ii) a bicameral legislature
    iii) a ceremonial executive head of state
    iv) Douala as the administrative capital.

Even though at the tripartite conference in Buea of 15-17 May 1961 the Ahmadou Ahidjo regime in Yaoundé agreed that unification would be on a federal basis, Ahmadou Ahidjo's own personal

---

[29]CO554/2258 XC 4122 of 15th June, 1961.
[30]PRO CO 554/2260 of 11th August, 1961.
[31]Ibid.
[32]Prior to the meetings at Foumban in 1961.

position was that the republican form of the regime would not change: "…the republic … had to transform itself into a federation, taking into account *the return* to it of a part of its territory…. The question therefore was not one of the birth of a new Republic with a federal form."[33]

By means of an alternative diplomacy, *La République du Cameroun* stifled the sovereign status of the Southern Cameroons to make her an *acquired additional* territory of herself. Verily, today, the Southern Cameroons is part of *La République du Cameroun*.   Should the Southern Cameroons continue to be part of *La République du Cameroun*?

The Southern Cameroons and *La République du Cameroun* were supposed to be sovereign entities in some sort of federation. Southern Cameroonians might have to DECIDE [choose again]. How do we get to the point where Southern Cameroonians will be consulted?

The UN can be thought to be responsible for the present situation of conflict in the Southern Cameroons. The provision in the UN Charter regarding union between countries is that if one of those countries is a member state of the UN as *La République du Cameroun* was, it has to agree with the territory it wished to join. Necessarily, this involves a signed treaty by the two countries wishing to unite, and a copy of the treaty deposited in evidence at the UN Secretariat in New York. It is stated in Article 102/103 of the UN Charter that if the two parties do not submit their written intentions of joining to the Secretariat of the UN against receipt, what they have done is invalid by virtue of the UN Constitutional Provision: "No party to any such treaty or international agreement which has not been registered in accordance with the provisions of paragraph 1 of Article 102 may invoke that treaty or agreement before any of the six organs of the UN." The UN left the territory under its tutelage to be annexed by *La République du Cameroun*. She did not supervise the July 1961 meetings of Foumban as much as she did not remind *La République du Cameroun* of its duty to respect Resolution 1605(xv).

Should the international community impose a union on the Southern Cameroons? Can they do that? *La République du Cameroun* is banking on its claim that, the Southern Cameroons never attained the rank of a sovereign entity and so is not an equal in International Law. That is only a claim though. Actually, *La Republique du Cameroun* on purpose, decided to ignore the UN vote on the independence of the Southern Cameroons, and Resolution 1605(xv).

The African Union, the Commonwealth and a number of other international organisations including influential nations around the world, in acknowledgement of the claims to sovereignty of the Southern Cameroons, have proposed a dialogue between *La République du Cameroun* and the Southern Cameroons. But a dialogue over what? The atrocities of the war declared by the personnel in power in *La République du Cameroun* against the peoples of the Southern Cameroons, speak loudly for what it stands, namely, domination and control of the Southern Cameroons. They would kill everyone! Inspiration for this can definitely be traced to the pogroms[34] carried out by France in the Sanaga-Maritime Region in 1955-1958 to ensure the station of Cameroun as a district of France after a supposed accession to independence. A dialogue and talks will never get off the table.

Garbage in! Garbage out! The leadership of *Cameroon* today, in relation to the Anglophone problem, find themselves in the same situation as the French yesterday, in relation to decolonisation and independence for the mandated territory of Cameroon. Perhaps French

---

[33] As told by *Ahmadou Ahidjo*, 1958-1968, (Paul Bory Publishing Monaco, February 1968), p. 34.

[34] Carried out by fighters – including non-Camerounese forces from neighbouring countries – armed and trained by France, and receiving on the spot instructions from the personnel the French had installed as its administrators in the so said independent *Republique du Cameroun*, and who are still in power today.

decolonisation was a success despite the cost for the opponents of the French scheme and for Cameroon. Everyone is watching.

CONCLUSION

The state which cannot find the right strategies to reconcile the conflicting interests that it tries to rule, loses legitimacy in the eyes of the population; it fails in its task and the justification for its existence becomes blurred.

According to Swartz, Turner, and Tuden (1966), politics is the way power is *achieved* and *used* to create and implement public goals. Those to whom the right to power is delegated are said to have authority, the legitimate right to power or to threaten the use of force to achieve such goals. It is through its political system that a society exercises power to maintain order internally and to regulate its relations with other societies.

Political scientists theorise on how power may be delegated, and make a distinction between the legitimate *use* of power and illegitimate *use* of power. Government for instance, is not legitimate if it is not carried on with the consent of the governed. Legitimacy is the basis of such governmental power as is exercised, both with an awareness on the government's part that it has a right to govern, and with some acknowledgment by the governed of that right (Dolf, 1968). In the jargon of political scientists we have what they call constitutional governance – governance based on a system of rules chosen at an earlier period; and democratic governance – governance characterised by a significant level of transparency and accountability and by full and effective participation of popular forces. "The basis of constitutional legitimacy must be measured by the extent to which the masses were part of the process of compacting the constitution."[1]

In political systems, at all times, there is a tendency for subordinates to reject the authority of superiors. These on the other hand are held in check by forces of legitimacy – widespread operation of forces, which engender a belief in the worthiness of the authority structure. Legitimacy and its entropic opposite are in tension such that any increase in one equals a decrease in the other.

The question of legitimacy of the leadership which negotiated the *conditional* independence granted by France to French Cameroun on the 1st January 1960, and the so-called *re*-unification with Southern British Cameroons is probably the single question which would not wish itself away. Mostly, we think of legitimacy together with the ability to govern: how much legitimacy would one attribute to a government when an entire section of the governed would not consider it as an authority on so important an issue as the issue of education and the courts? Parents would not send their children to school, and lawyers would not resume their activity on the terms of the State! And openly and with undoubted enthusiasm the streets would identify with the call for boycott of the state. We think that such a government would execute itself!

A healthy march on for *La République du Cameroon* (2017-) cannot be without a thought through revisiting of this issue. Driven by the prospects of personal gains as this obviously was the case for the French-chosen spokesmen of a people the French manifestly considered and dealt with as one would deal with *lesser* beings [not quite humans], the basis of the *vivre ensemble* that is often invoked any time the system experiences a hiccup could hardly have been sufficiently pondered, that, it would stand the test of change as it is the situation of every constituted system.

---

[1] Submission credited to Femi Falana, President of the Committee for the Defense of Human Rights, Lagos Nigeria on June 23rd 1999 in George Clay Kieh, Pita Ogaba Agbese (Eds.) (2014). *Reconstructing the authoritarian state in Africa*. London and New York: Routledge. Pp. 18-53.

Cameroonians wish to understand how one can be the president of a country and declare war on his people; what laws to define the event and the punishment of those who betrayed, tortured, humiliated, impoverished them and brag about the genocide that they commit in the country. They desire to discuss how never again to fall in such a nightmare of a trap and together, define the best system of order.[2]

They have already condemned Monsieur Paul Biya and his collaborators. Would he leave office? Perhaps go into exile. Can he anymore? The dictator prospers in disorder, the humiliation and despair of his people, before he slumps into murders and especially into obsession with a way out for himself. The killings, and the extent of blood that has been spilt! The point of no return seems to have been attained: he is either in power of he dies in power even if it gets to the worst of general chaos. It is time up for this two times confiscator of the victory of a people: it is over for the tyrant. The single item for dialogue if it ever gets to that, is the extent of their magnanimity with regard to the punishment to be meted out which is anything from just retiring the culprits, to hanging pure and simple. Hopefully, the heroes of independence for *La République du Cameroun* will soon finally get a popper burial and there would be closure for hundreds of thousands who were traumatised by the killings of this little man and his predecessor!

On the ongoing war pitting *La République du Cameroun* and the Southern Cameroons, Monsieur Paul Biya and his collaborators it would seem to many an analyst, are not relevant anymore. The so-called visits to the Southern Cameroons [...] for peace and the supposed dialogue organised as a consequence of the visits smack mostly of some Don Quixote events! It is interesting that this learned gentleman [the Prime Minister of *La République francophone du Cameroun*] does not see it that way – that any a reasonable Southern Cameroonian would not without qualms, accept to be the ambassador and spokesperson [mostly in the role of the fiddle], this time around, of a regime so affected by the qualification of brutality and killings. The least that can be entertained at this point in time is that the so-called forces of defense and security and the annexor administration loyal to *La République du Cameroun* are recalled to their country. The international community[3] has to return to its responsibility of restituting to the Southern Cameroons its duly earned rights to sovereignty.

---

[2] Source: https://mobile.cameroonweb.com/CameroonHomePage/NewsArchive/S-rail-doutes-sur-le-dialogue-annonc-entre-Biya-et-les-s-paratistes-462935

[3] 14th of December 1960 UN General Assembly Resolution 1514(XV) that all countries of the world would be granted unconditional independence, so that their peoples could exercise their liberty as free citizens.

BIBLIOGRAPHY

Anyangwe, C. (2008). "Imperialist politics in Cameroon: Resistance and the inception of the restoration of the statehood of southern Cameroons" pp. 60 - 70.

Ashcraft, Richard (ed.) (1991), *John Locke: critical assessments*. London: Routledge.

Bouamama, Saïd. FUIQP cours n^{o3}_Ruben Um Nyobe_ le Mpodol (porte-parole) (WWW search). Date accessed: 08/04/2016.

Cole, A. and Raymond, G. (2006). *Redefining the French republic*. Manchester: Manchester University Press.

Dolf, Sternberger, (1968). "Legitimacy" in *International Encyclopaedia of the Social Sciences* (ed. D. L. Sills) Vol. 9 (p. 244). New York: Macmillan.

Domergue M., Tatsitsa J. and Deltombe T. (2011). *Kamerun! Histoire d'une guère cachée*. Paris: La Découverte. WWW search: Date accessed: 30/06/2014.

Donnat, Gaston. "Algérie-Cameroun-Afrique." *Mémoire Africaine:* Harmattan.

Ebune J. B. (1992). *Growth of political parties in Southern British Cameroons, 1916-1960*. Yaoundé: Centre d'édition et de production pour l'enseignement et la recherche.

Fanon, Frantz (1959). *Les damnés de la terre*. Published by Pelican. Speech to Congress of Black African Writers.

Förster, S., Wolfgang J. Mommsen, and Ronald Edward Robinson. (1989). *Bismarck, Europe, and Africa: The Berlin Africa Conference 1884-1885 and the Onset of Partition*. Oxford: Oxford University Press.

Hobson, I. A. (1965). *Imperialism: a study*. Ann Arbor: University of Michigan Press.

http://www.ambazonia.org/index.php?option=com_content&view=article&id=249:jua-Ahmadou Ahidjo-tug-of-war&catid=63:politics&Itemid=261

https://www.youtube.com/watch?v=cRLhqNPVZ4Y

Joseph, Richard (Ed.) (1978). *Gaullist Africa: Cameroon under Ahmadou Ahidjo*. Enugu: Fourth Dimension Publishers.

Joseph, Richard, (1977). *Radical nationalism in Cameroon: social origins of the U.P.C. rebellion*. Oxford: Oxford University Press.

Kale P. M. (1967). *Political evolution in the Cameroons*. Buea: Government Printers.

Konings, P. and Nyamjoh, F. B. (1997). "The anglophone problem in Cameroon." In the *Journal of Modern African Studies*, 35, 2 pp.207-229.

le Roy, Gaëlle et Valérie Osouf. "Cameroun Autopsie d'une pseudo indépendance."UN film écrit et réalisé par WWW search accessed on12/07/2016.

Mamdani, Mahmood "The question of justice in response to political violence." WWW search accessed on 12/07/ 2016

Mbaku, John Mukum (2014). "The state and Cameroon's stalled transition to democratic governance" in George Clay Kieh, Pita Ogaba Agbese (Eds.) (2014). *Reconstructing the authoritarian state in Africa*. London and New York: Routledge. Pp. 18 – 53.

Mbembe, Achille (1966). *La naissance du maquis dans le Sud-Cameroun*. Paris: Karthala.

Mintoogue, Yves. "La mort de Ruben Um Nyobe" (https://mintoogue N° 9 WWW Search). Date accessed: 10/01/2017.

Mongo Beti (1972). *Main basse sur le Cameroun: Autopsie d'une décolonisation*. Paris: La Découverte.

Nkosi, Sibusiso (2005). *Mzimela*. Annual Conference of Pan African Anthropological Association.

Swartz, M. J., Turner, V. W. and Tuden, A. (eds.) (1966). *Political anthropology*. Chicago Aldine.

The Saylor Foundation, "Overview of politics in the post-colonial era" The Saylor Foundation POLSC325-Sub-Unit-2.1. (WWW Search). Date accessed:14/01/2017.

Tobner, Odile. "Guerre au Cameroun_histoire d'une censure obstinée et persistante" - ODILE TOBNER (youtube www search). Date accessed : 05/04/2016.

Um Nyobe, Ruben (1984). *Le problème national kamerunais*. Paris: L'Harmattan.

www.kamerun-lesite.org ND.

Table of Contents

More
Books!

OMNIScriptum

Printed by Books on Demand GmbH, Norderstedt / Germany